# What

Parkinson's disease is a cruel and unrelenting visitor and my friend Mike Potts has battled this internal monster for almost 15 yrs now. When I was 11 years old Mike was a young pastoral intern at the church I attended. At summer camp Mike explained the Gospel to me and I gave my life to Christ. From that point on I knew I wanted to be like Mike Potts, he was young, cool and sold out to Christ. That was almost 35 years ago. Now I pastor a church where Mike is a deacon and I watch his struggle up close. I see the weight of his disease and the Gospel driven determination that keeps him going. Thirty Five years later I still find myself wanting to be like Mike Potts. This book stands as a testimony to God's grace in the midst of a life of struggle. Mikes' story gives ample evidence that behind every dark cloud is a smiling Providence and what appears to be evil, in the hands of God, is intended for good. Read this book and be inspired by hope in the midst of despair.

—Clint Pressley, Senior Pastor of
Hickory Grove Baptist Church,
Charlotte, North Carolina

Few men can face the trials and difficulties of this life, as did Joseph in the Bible. But I would add to that list, the author of this book, Michael Potts. But there is one difference between the two. Joseph had his trials at the early part of his life, and then he became second in command of the nation of Egypt. Michael Potts has had his trials in the later years of his life. Previously, he had been a very successful pastor, who had served several large churches over the years, and he had spoken in many places! But then came the devastating plague of Parkinson's disease! And this could have been a devastation many men would never overcome! But in this book, Michael Potts uses the life of Joseph, alongside of his own life, to set forth many truths for those who face suffering and sorrow and seeming defeat in their days on this earth. The reader will come to see, something of the grace and purpose of God, even as one, while on earth, passes through the greatest of trials possible!

—Dr. Richard P. Belcher,
Retired Professor of Columbia
International University, Columbia, SC

"My dear and longtime friend, Mike wrote a true and gut-wrenching book, that is challenging and inspiring to everyone. It made me take another look at my life and how I deal with adversity and God in general."

—Bernhard Langer, PGA Golf Professional

When you open up and read *Living in the Meanwhile*, you're actually looking into a life...a life I've been privileged to personally know and which I now see through the lens of God's redemptive power. With heartfelt honesty and heroic bravery, Mike opens up his chest and invites us to look inside. He shares his darkest hours and deepest fears with us, because they assure as nothing else can when we see the Lord glorified through them. Regardless of what your "meanwhile" is, this book will provide the perspective and prescription you need to experience the surpassing power and peace of God.

—Pastor Bob Coy
Calvary Chapel of Fort Lauderdale

# LIVING
## in the
# MEANWHILE

# LIVING
## in the
# MEANWHILE

MICHAEL POTTS

TATE PUBLISHING
AND ENTERPRISES, LLC

Published by Tate Publishing & Enterprises, LLC
127 E. Trade Center Terrace | Mustang, Oklahoma 73064 USA
1.888.361.9473 | www.tatepublishing.com

Tate Publishing is committed to excellence in the publishing industry. The company reflects the philosophy established by the founders, based on Psalm 68:11,
*"The Lord gave the word and great was the company of those who published it."*

Published in the United States of America

ISBN: 978-1-62994-078-6
1. Biography & Autobiography / Personal Memoirs
2. Religion / Christian Life / Inspirational
13.11.25

# Dedication


To Linda, my life.

To Trevor and his wife, Katherine, Tyler and Ashleigh, my joy.

Thank you with all my heart for walking with me through this *meanwhile*.

# Acknowledgments

A special thank-you goes out from my heart to: my mother who, at eighty-eight, is still my cheerleader in life, my dad who, if was living, still would have been so proud, my wife's parents, Dave and Pat Bardin, for all your love throughout the years.

Dick and Barbara, who remind me there are those who stay closer than a brother (and sister).

Gary and Cecilia Peters, for your consistent support, Wes, Ron, and Clint, who walk with me in Christ while keeping me grounded in his word.

The members of my Sunday School class at Hickory Grove Baptist Church, thank you for your excitement and joy.

Dr. Tatter, my hero, you gave me my life back.

Pastor Bob Coy, you are the best of the best pastor/teacher that I know.

Bernhard, you are absolutely the definition of what it means to be a friend.

Jim, we share the same path as we fight Parkinson's...keep the Ft. Lauderdale office open! Mark, you never stopped believing in me.

Dale and Joanne, Steve and Sue, Bryan and Margaret, Gene and Caryn, Johnny and Dawn, Mike and JoAnn you are friends for life.

Krystil, who labored over presenting a readable manuscript.

Dr. Belcher, you push and inspire me to finish well, and to the many family and friends who have been such a support as we all learn how to live in the meanwhile.

# Contents

# Preface

Nothing ticks me off more than to hear or read accounts of people's struggles and how God molded their character through the times of trial. Then, they write or speak about how they are now living large in the big city, having a large bank account and a pain-free existence. To top it all off, they tell me they have a burden for those who are where they have been. Well, thank you very much, but what I want to read is an authentic account of life while life is not seemingly making sense. How are they coping when life stinks? And I mean *really* stinks. How am I to believe the blessing will come when God seems so removed? How am I to exist when I am suffocating from a lack of spiritual breath? I want the testimony in the midst, not after they have landed a spot on Oprah.

This craving for realness has led me to write this book. I have Parkinson's disease, and I don't like it. Like Joseph, I am on a caravan to Egypt, and most days seem like hell. I am living not with a mere diagnosis, but with a lifestyle. I am living in the "meanwhile," a concept I will explore with those who care to know how to live—really live. So, if you are ready for the truth of realness, you will discover a depth of life that goes beyond the marketing of God. *Living in the Meanwhile* cultivates an authenticity of faith that leads one to a magnified contentment in the midst of life's challenges. I know; I am there.

# The Pain Realized

It was supposed to be a routine visit to a specialist just to check out what was thought to be a pinched nerve. My buddies from home picked me up at the Charlotte Airport and off we drove to Duke University Hospital. I lured them with the hope that afterwards, we would land a spot at a barbecue restaurant, North Carolina style. Dick, Dave, and I had always been there for each other. We had celebrated the wedding joys of our respective marriages, stood by Dick during the dark days of the tragic death of his parents in a car accident in New Mexico ten years earlier, celebrated anniversaries together, and applauded the arrival of our children through birth and adoption. (But like true friends, we forgot each other's birthdays.) So, it was just natural that we made the ride together to Duke. The distraction was barbecue.

We made our way down the confusing hallways of Duke, carrying the burden of x-rays, MRIs, and test results.

"How do you feel?" they said, knowing that was a loaded question to someone who cries at the same spot in *Little Giants*, *Rudy*, and *Gone with the Wind* no matter how many times I've seen them.

"Fine," I said, but in the back of my mind, I hesitated with the thought, *What if…? What if it was not?* But I quickly denied it. Barbeque—North Carolina barbecue was my goal. Deep-fried hush puppies and sweet iced tea—something I was denied in South Florida.

We had to sit quietly in the lobby, so we tried to act civil by appearing to read, but just like in high school, we people watched and cracked on just about everybody who walked through the neurological lobby doors. Just as I was appearing to be reading—

"Mr. Potts…this way please."

I rose quickly but cautiously and followed my guide down to the examination room where *he* stood, waiting. He—being the very bookish-looking doctor—who, I later learned, had no bedside manner or was not even aware of the need for it. He was the sort of doctor who, to be as kind as I can be, was a legend in his own mind. He most likely didn't like people, so he opted to lecture rather than practice on people…and I did say practice.

I went through the routine of tapping my feet and fingers and touching my nose with my eyes shut. It was much like the sideshow of the police and the drunk. Then, he left without a word. Upon his return, twenty minutes later no less, he looked distracted yet to the point. With reading glasses halfway down his nose, he said words I feared and worked hard not to ever accept—words that would alter my life forever.

"Mr. Potts, I am sorry to tell you, but you have Parkinson's disease."

Just for a moment, time stood still.

"Excuse me?" I said, hoping those two small words would be enough to awaken me from what I hoped would be only a distraction from the barbecue.

"Uh—you have Parkinson's."

Now you have to understand, I was then and had always been the golden boy, born an only child. I never strayed in life except one time when I took some puffs on a cigarette in the woods with Tex Caulder (which I later confessed because I thought I would go to hell or would have to endure my mother's wrath, which—at twelve years old—*seemed* like hell). So, when he said Parkinson's, it really didn't register with me.

"We normally don't put people on medication this early, but you will eventually be on medication because you will get worse. However, there is a drug that would reduce your symptoms by 60 percent."

"Well then, why wouldn't you put me on it now?" I questioned.

"Okay," he said, "if you insist."

By this time, it was very clear to me that this guy was a jerk—an educated jerk, but a jerk nonetheless. Yet jerk or no jerk, I can still hear those words as if it were hours ago I first heard them. "You have Parkinson's disease; come back in six weeks." He departed, and I never returned.

I sat alone in that cold, stoic examination room for what felt like hours, but in reality, it was no more than five minutes. *So that's it*, I pondered, *I have Parkinson's disease. God, if this is some type of providential humor or some test of my wearing thin faith, then now would be a good time to stop it. I mean really, I am forty-five, have a beautiful wife, three kids, a dog named Ruffles, and a fish named Caryn. And in case you have had a relapse in your sovereignty, I am a preacher.* As if that title scotch guarded my life from pain. Up to this point, I had been basically pain-free, except when I was not elected Valentine King alongside Rhonda Thomas in sixth grade. This was worse by far.

*Get a grip, Michael.* And I did. But getting a grip without processing my newfound news would prove to be the impetus to the growing fear, doubt, anger, and disillusionment that would bury me later. Then again, Christians often get a grip without processing pain and then later fall apart and blame it all on Satan. Granted, Satan is not a nice guy, but he gets credit for a lot of our pain that caught him by as much of a surprise as it did us.

I gathered my hands full of test results and walked back to the lobby where Dick and Dave were waiting. They could tell I was shaken.

"It's not a pinched nerve," Dick said reluctantly.

"No," I said, holding back the explosion of emotions that would later come out. "It's not."

We knew that Parkinson's was a possibility, but we never allowed it to dominate the list of solutions.

"Yes, it's…it's Parkin." My voice broke.

"Let's walk," Dave said.

And walk we did to the Duke Chapel. The Duke Chapel is a gothic cathedral on the Duke campus that, to some, is a mere piece of ornate architecture, but for me became my first haven of rest in this disturbing journey. We walked down the left side to the third row from the front and sat down. As I reached out to touch my pain bearers, all three of us cried like babies. The barbecue could wait.

As we drove out of the Duke parking lot, I began to realize that the impact of the last few hours would now begin to dictate the rest of the journey of my life. As a Christian, I knew all the standard words of comfort, but the reality of unwanted pain will always seek to control the moment. Now, on an early June morning in 2001, the pain was at my door, threatening the very comfort zone in which I'd been living my life. I called Linda from the car and gave her the news. With her usual control of emotions, she responded, "Well, it's not what we prayed for, but we will make it."

I have learned after twenty years of marriage that Linda is stoic, and I am explosive. Nobody knows the pain she was going through with fear of the unknown. I had Dick and Dave with me, but on the other end of the phone stood one who, in the midst of supper plans, had to deal with this altering news. So, if the words *we will make it* sound calculated, they were, but for the moment, they were her survival. It would be months later before the emotions would cause the curves in her life—the same curves I, in the impending months, was about to meet in the darkness of the night.

To keep my promise, the attention had to turn to something more filling, so we settled for Lexington Barbecue and ate 'til we could not stuff another hush puppy into our awaiting mouths. If hush puppies could cure Parkinson's, then I would have been healed that night! Every so often, I would reflect upon the negative; the "what if," but Dick and Dave made sure I focused on living through this ordeal and staying positive and focused on God.

The first test would come hours later when I drove up into my parents' driveway to face their denial that anything was wrong with me. But then again, they are parents (something I understand more as my own children get older). As the night ended, I lay alone with my body, soul, and spirit stretched out before God. *Where did I go wrong? What did I do?* These questions revealed a moment of amnesia of what grace is all about, a subject that was a constant theme of my preaching. Then my questions turned to more spiritual reflection, yet were somewhat overly bold. *Where were you, God, on some unknown day when the elements were allowed to inflict my body with the Parkinson's?* All the images of the extreme symptoms were played out. I remembered seeing Robin Williams's movie, *Awakenings*, several years earlier about the discovery of a Parkinson's-related disease and its treatment, thinking how awful it was. And now, here I was with Parkinson's, staring me cold in the face. I was a successful preacher, had a radio ministry, a growing church, and an active family with sons excelling in sports. I had waited so long to be the emotional father, running on the sidelines or walking the fairways. Then there was Ashleigh, my daughter, four years old at the time. Would I walk her down the aisle someday? Ultimately, there was Linda. We are eleven years apart. I married the girl of my dreams, but would I be there for her, and would she still want me? You say how absurd to think such thoughts, but it's not to those in pain. The fear of the stilling night is very real. Would the morning really bring joy, or would it merely offer up an ever-growing stiff body and trembling lips? I had often quoted Psalm 30 to and for others, but now I had to live it. In the later months, this Psalm would be used by God to lead me into a recovery from depression. But for now, it was, well, a nice gesture of God's sovereignty.

I lay there that night, thinking of what tomorrow would bring. I was not sure, but I knew my life would not be the same. Little did I know how different it would become. The plane ride back to South Florida was long, reflective, and proved to be the beginning of a journey yet to end.

## Unwanted Pain

The pain was sifted into my life,
Reaching the very innermost part of my soul
Unexpecting
Attacking
Lingering
The pain was jolted into my memory
Causing the very fibers of my body to explode
Wondering
Imagining
Questioning
The pain resides in my experience

Attacking the very moments of time
Fearing
Unsettling
Controlling
The pain now belongs to me
Pushing the very joy of my life
Diminishing
Punishing
Yet deserving
This pain sifted, jolted, resided, belonged
Unwanted yet allowed
Shaping
Guiding
Providing…
A new beginning.

# The Breaking

It was supposed to be a routine task of taking food supplies to his brothers. Collectively, they were tending the sheep some distance away in Shechem and were later found some thirteen miles farther north in Dothan. The story unfolds in Genesis 37 when Jacob's youngest son Joseph was sent to his brothers. The question that comes to mind is why wasn't Joseph already with them? He was seventeen, certainly ready to take on shepherding with his brothers. But his absence is not about Joseph. In the course of sibling rivalry, Joseph was clearly the favored son. No doubt in the backroom talks his brothers had, there was a silent mocking: "Joseph this, Joseph that. When will the old man let up?" But, the family contention had all started with the dreams. Joseph had two dreams. In each one he had casted himself as superior over his older brothers. They indeed would bow down to him one day. This of course did not settle well with his older brothers and even his father, Jacob was taken aback by his young son's arrogance. When I think of the very tense family meeting when Joseph informed them of his dreams, the first thing that comes to mind is why in the world you would share such thoughts with your already jealous brothers. Even the loving father could be pushed to far. Then there was the robe. Joseph had been fitted with an ornate robe that carried with it the mark of favoritism from the father. To the brothers, the robe was a daily reminder that they did not quite measure up to the attention of their father. The soon to be obvious emotional war, between Joseph and his brothers started with a deep-seeded jealousy that led to an unforgiving hatred toward Joseph. The growing tension between the brothers and Joseph was also a growing bitterness to punish the father who had favored Joseph to the point that when men go out to war little boys stay home and Joseph was still a little boy in the eyes of Jacob.

To put it in modern day vernacular, Joseph was a brat—a rich, authenticated brat. Joseph, no doubt, was like Ferris Bueller in the movie *Ferris Bueller's Day Off*. There's that engrossing moment when Ferris decides to stay home from school and rule the world. This was Joseph par excellence. His brothers had already stomached the nauseating thought of his dreams of superiority. Once again, Jacob, the father, was passive. The Bible says, "He pondered these things in his heart." That is a nice way of saying he wimped out. He was what we would call a dysfunctional father; raising twelve sons and one daughter as a single father, having had the girl of his dreams die. I am sure he had the best intentions, but at the end of the day, what does a little dream matter anyway?

Let's face it, we are all dysfunctional. It is called sin nature. This movement of dysfunctionalism was not discovered in some governmental think tank on human psyche. God called it when he asked Adam in the garden, "Why are you hiding from me?" We all have fig leaves on, just some were made by Polo or Hugo Boss and others were bought at the thrift store with the labels cutout. However, in the final hour, they all have to be washed with the same eternal cleansing. So, when Jacob did not confront his strong-willed child, we understand. But understanding doesn't change the fact that this prideful yet ambitious young man would have to be broken in order for God to live out his potential in Joseph. Joseph would indeed rule the world one day, yet prior to his crowning moment, Joseph would see God strip him of more than a robe.

I'll come back to the robe later.

I have two teenage boys as well as an eight-year-old girl. The boys are so different. One is so aggressive and forceful—to call him strong-willed is too soft. But he is caring and passionate. He can make you cry, and a minute later have you rolling hysterically from some off-the-wall comment. I love him because one day, he will rule his world. God has a plan, but right now, my son is in process (not to mention on a little medication). He wears his robe well, but one day, I know God will strip it from him like he has mine more than once. As with Joseph, God is in the business of breaking his people in order to prepare them for the next adventure in life. The breaking is always painful, but also always leads to the unveiling of the unexpectable plans of God in our lives and the untapped power he desires to uncover in our everyday experiences. This hope lures us into the "meanwhile" of God (which is the message of Joseph), where we find our sustaining power in the midst of our journey of faith.

The meanwhile will be explained later...

So, in the course of providential history, God had to break a struggling teenager in such a way to prepare him to be a type of Christ in the Old Testament. This was to lead him to become a provider for the people of Israel in order to carry out the scarlet thread of redemption. One day, this redemption would embody itself in the person of Christ and bring the climactic moment when the Father of creation would proclaim, "It is finished." Just think, it had its earliest beginnings in a favored son's life in the middle of Hebron—a son who was grossly misunderstood by his family, yet who somehow knew his life would be lived to a different beat. Amazing the similarities to another preteen in Hebron hundreds of years later who was also misunderstood by his family yet knew that his life would be about his father's business. His name was Jesus, who was ultimately broken, not for his own shortcomings, but for yours and mine.

So the drama continues with stored up emotions as the brothers saw Joseph coming. Maybe the sun came down just right on the coat with the colors, showing off with mysterious brightness. It was the symbol of preferential treatment. Maybe the colors stood bold as the brothers confronted their fight for self-worth. Whatever can be said, the fact was that deep down inside, each of the bands of brothers wore bitterness on his sleeves. This was the moment to appease their anger because yes, the dream was ever before them. With a malicious spirit, they must have said, "Here comes that dreamer," not knowing their bitterness would lead them down the road of premeditated murder. This would be their chance to avenge their sleepless nights of feeling unaccepted and unworthy in the eyes of their father. It was an unhealthy relationship at best. But could they, would they actually get rid of their emotional assassin? This was a defining moment, and what they decided was that self-survival would prevail. They had forgotten one thing, however. Whatever could be said about his arrogance, Joseph was their brother. So it was with a family benevolence that big brother Rueben brought forth a satisfying solution: throw him in a pit and simulate a tragic accident. One step closer, their adrenaline began to work overtime, and before they knew it, Joseph was abandoned with joy by throwing him in an open pit. The amazing thing to me is that the Bible says they sat down to eat afterwards. Just picture it with me. The brothers all sat with playful grins as they heard their young dreamer squeal, "Come on, guys, wait 'til Dad finds out." I am sure with laughter they responded, "Dream on, little brother." Little did they know, he would. For in that pit that day birthed a new work of God in Joseph's life. You see, God had to get Joseph to Egypt in order to carry out his covenantal plan for Israel. God chose not to engage in a plan of enticement. Instead, he chose the evil intent of the brothers to be the conduit for a new work of his drama with man. His ultimate plan was at this point clouded, though.

I arrived back to Ft. Lauderdale to be welcomed by a sea of concerns and tears by my many friends. Linda was a rock and kept my mind from straying. She is the eternal fix-it master, so research on Parkinson's became her hobby. What foods to eat and what supplements to take was at the forefront of her agenda. I was quite disinterested because dealing with it meant that I had to admit it, and I was not ready for that.

The following Sunday morning, I met with the elders in our executive directors of ministries office at the church I had pastored for almost ten years. I informed them that it was a diagnosis of Parkinson's disease, early stages, and I assured them I had many more sermons left in me. The room was still, motionless, and unresponsive at first. I had stood with most of them in some crises in their lives. We had seen this bankrupt ministry come back to life through our collective efforts and God's faithfulness. The struggling 400 plus congregation had grown to around 1,600 and a staff close to 60. The reactions were different, but the one comment that would actually begin to haunt me was, "I am sorry to hear it, but will you be preaching next Sunday, and when will you tell the congregation?" I normally lived in a Wizard of Oz mentality, and I guess I thought it would have been nice to hear them say something like, "Take some time off." But one of the gatekeepers of the ministry reminded me that I had very little vacation left, unless, of course, I wanted to take time off without pay. Today, I am sure they do not remember that, but I do. For the most part, they were supportive. The two I worried most about were the self-appointed boy scouts of the church. These two had dutifully embraced me when they first came to the church, but over time, their theological disenchantment of me became very verbalized and confrontational. I remember how one of them sought me out at a board meeting I was attending some twenty minutes away from the church.

"I have to talk to you," he said.

The pastor in me wanted to allow this for I feared something wrong in his voice; perhaps his marriage or his kids, but it took only one comment to soon realize he was out to do theological battle over how I shared the gospel. My approach, it seemed, was too inclusive of the whole world to war well with what he said was a true Calvinist. His passion for theological exactness was really a misplaced zeal for form rather than substance, for a system rather than balanced truth. His brand of Calvinism was not Calvinism at all but rather an attitude of theological arrogance. So, in this vein, he stated his claim.

"You cannot tell people that Jesus loves them," he said.

"Really?" I asked, baiting him to later see him bury himself in theological and philosophical unreasonableness.

"Oh, you see, if you tell someone that Jesus loves them and he has not chosen them, then you have lied to them."

Now I guess somewhere there is logic in all that, but logic never outweighs the mystery of God. The mystery is that only God knows the chosen, and I am to pray and preach as if to compel all men to Christ because it is all up to God. God is the keeper of the keys, not man. How presumptuous of man! My friend is sincere but sincerely wrong—at best, out of balance. If he would only realize how embarrassing his arrogance is in the face of grace!

Those with theological extremes will eventually embarrass themselves because they cannot live consistent with their view, and any philosophy major knows this is the test of truth. The view always breaks at this point and one is left to drift in a sea of relativism which is the very thing that my friend and others, like him, fight against. So, when I asked him how he knew he was saved, he said it was because Jesus died for his sin. I then asked him what if he got to heaven and God said, "I know you tried, and you gained a lot of knowledge about me and even taught about me, but I am sorry. I don't have you on my list."

"He would not do that," he retorted.

At this point, he slipped into the abyss of personal opinion, and his argument failed. I have chosen to take this sidebar to share this theological battle I encountered because there are those in the Calvinistic camp who seek to wordsmith to the point of dutifully taking the heart right out of the gospel. It seems to me that Jesus talked about those of this fervor when he called them "white washed tombs," appearing to be alive but, in fact, dead. Why? Because there is no fruit of the Spirit evident and that is the test of conversion, not theological exactness. They love the truth of God and books, but they do not love people. And let there be no mistake, Jesus died for people, not institution or man-made camps of theology. You see, this is their robe, and it must be stripped or they will be left with dead orthodoxy and empty pews. As my southern mother would say, "Bless their hearts." These are good men, and I respect their knowledge, but their hearts so lacks grace, a hallmark of the gospel they so valiantly seek to protect. Little did they know that the pit they began to dig for me would, like with Joseph, be the impetus for God to do a new work in me.

The pit for me became a headlong dive into a depression which was to be new ground for me, but I have come to understand that depression is common with early onset Parkinson's. In order to express that day in the staff member's office, the power of the pen moves me to simply say that something died in my soul that only now, five years removed, begins to be resurrected. The dark chamber of a seared hope will seek to harden our outer shell until the kiss of God's peace begins to breakthrough. As with Joseph, the imprisonment of my emotions would indeed become the encampment of a newly crafted future in order to allow my dreams to live again. Joseph was in the meanwhile and so was I. The kiss of God was yet to come.

But let us go back to Joseph where we left him, in the pit. Imagine Joseph, who was used to having full control of his surroundings, now encased within a darkened tomb. His thoughts must have varied, perhaps anticipating the brothers' hopeful practical joke to be over. The Bible says the pit was empty of water which tells us that it was an abandoned well. The image is thick with emotions as well as spiderwebs, crawling insects, mildew, and an earthen stench, far removed from the comfortable surroundings of his Hebron home. He soon realized that this was not a brief joke of brotherly fun. As he heard the plans beginning to unfold, he must have started fearing the worst. The worst, of course, was God's best.

The best would come through the awaiting arrival of an Eastern caravan. Every time I read this account, it still throws me beyond imagination to think that the brothers could sit there and eat (while awaiting the grand entrance of the strangers from the East) without slipping off to a regretful stare that they had done something wrong. Indeed, they had, but they kept on eating. Somewhere along the flow of ever-increasing guilt, their plan turned into a premeditated murder plot with an unbridled hatred. You might choose to call it merely a sibling rivalry thing, but this was the expression of true dislike. I do not think it really crossed Joseph's mind that his brothers meant harm, real harm, until he heard the approaching hoof beats. He had heard their conversations as Judah spoke up, "What will we gain if we kill our own brother?"

*Okay. This is good, real good,* Joseph must have thought. *They're not going to kill me; I'll be getting out. They will joke around a little bit with the foreign traders about me and then this whole thing will be over. But I must admit that this time, they had me going. Thanks guys. Got the coat a little dirty, but do you hear me complaining? Upset? No way! I'll just be making my way back home to Dad.*

Judah continued, "Come, let us sell him to the Ishmaelites."

*Now, wait a minute. Did I hear "sell"? As in a slave, as in slavery, as in real work? You have got to be kidding me!*

Judah then played on the emotions of the family ties. "After all, he is our brother, our own flesh and blood."

*Good point. I am your bother, and that dream thing... well, I could have been wrong.*

I am sure Joseph must have had thoughts of regret. *If only I had kept my mouth shut about those dreams or at least not made such a big deal about them.*

Now, here is a good place to interject a few personal thoughts and reflect a moment on the practical side of faith. It seems that whenever we go through tough spots in life or crises, our first reaction is to look within ourselves and think "what if," or "I should have," as if our actions alone would interrupt the plans of God. Most who claim Christ as Savior and Lord have well-intentioned hearts about the practical implications of Christ's lordship, but when it comes down to the crunch of pain or discomfort, we still hold on to a notion that we can change it all in a matter of moments. The common avenue for change is seen as prayer. We engage in prayer and ask others to "agree with us in prayer." There were times as a local pastor that people would say to me, "Pastor Mike, would you please pray real hard?" about some issue in their lives. I often wondered (and still do) about how hard is hard enough. Then the question is, how do I know that I have prayed hard enough? I do not mean to make light of these sincere hearts, but we must be careful that we do not begin to believe that prayer is really twisting God's arm to get our way and that somewhere in the conversation with God, he cries "uncle," and we walk away happy and call it God's will. We must see that part of the breaking in life is giving over to God no matter what, thus seeing beyond the moments of life's ordeals. Being broken means that we accept the fact that sometimes God says no, and sometimes, subtle rebuke begs the question, "What part of *no* do you not understand?" At this point, we begin to see that God is beyond our human definition. Perhaps, Joseph was not thinking down this theological path, for he had never taken a theological course of study. I guarantee you, though, that he was feeling alone and no doubt, had been startled to hear the transaction of money and the wrestling of handshakes with the audible sounds of the word *sold* in the background. Broken, you say? No, shattered!

As the caravan began to pull away with his new travel companions, he must have begun to face the fact that not only had his travel plans been changed, but his whole life's itinerary had been altered. At some point, Joseph must have realized that these men he was now with were not his friends, but dare he admit—his owners. We are not told how long the journey to Egypt lasted or the specifics of his selling to Potiphar's household. But whatever happened that day in the slave market of Egypt, it was the apparent end of Joseph's life as he had known it.

Rueben returned and was somewhat dismayed. I say somewhat because Rueben was one of those "wannabe" leaders. He would lead if they would follow, but not if conditions weren't right. So, he expressed his concerns, but they were purely self-protective, aiming to make him come out looking unblemished in the eyes of his father. The Bible in Genesis 37:31-32 it says, "Then they got Joseph's robe and slaughtered a goat and dipped the robe in the blood. They took the robe back to their father and said, 'We found this. Examine it to see whether it is your son's robe.'" Notice how they removed themselves from any relationship with the robe or Joseph. He was their father's son, not their brother. Jacob replied, "It is my son's robe!" the grief was real and impacting but the coldness of the brothers was just as noticeably felt.

So there you have it. The brothers sought revenge, the father was broken and emotionally punished, and Joseph was gone...the end of a nice drama. Did I say Joseph gone? Yes, gone, but not out of their lives.

Where was God in all this? The question is legitimate and is one we all have in the back of our minds in the midst of our broken moments. There are times we are on a caravan to Egypt and life as we know it is seemingly over. The dark chambers of pain beg to bury our joy and hope, and what was once a heartfelt relationship with God is now cold and stoic. It seems we are left holding the bag of confusion. We are told in so many words in the normal church environment that we are not to question, just hold on like good little boys and girls and therefore bury our emotions. This type of faith keeps God on the outskirts of our lives, like a friend visiting from out of town, but it never allows him to live in our daily walk. We must wrestle with the question because, in asking the question, we find God in the middle of our wondering, and we are led to a wholeness that comes only through the broken moments. Life needs to be redefined for us, and before it can be, we must allow God to shatter our previous neatly packaged answers. What do we do when life does not seem to work? And for Joseph, life was not working.

Ultimately, this is the question of the heart for all of us. Joseph was not unique in his assumed struggle to understand life in the silent moments, but he is in fact the prototype of how to face brokenness even when brokenness occurs in the midst of the most unexpected of days.

My unexpected day would come months later, but for the moment, I piously called this plight I was facing, my adventure with God. To be honest, though, I must admit that I did not believe a word I was saying. I was, to be blunt, scared to death.

By the end of the summer of my June diagnosis of Parkinson's, I had managed to keep it all in with an occasional let-go of emotions (but nothing that made me appear weak). In times like this, there is one that sticks closer than a brother, and my friend Bernhard always called at the right moments with some word or gesture that kept me above the grave of despair. As a professional golfer, he knew the loneliness of silent hurting and the need to continue on in the public. Even today, I still do not know how he found the time to care for me, but he did and often would call me in the middle of a golf tournament just to say hi and that he loved me.

I remember one day so vividly when he called me on the phone to tell me he was going to meet me at the golf course to hit balls. I don't know if it was his concern for me or his German determination but, either way, he would not take no for an answer. So, off I went. You might say I should have jumped at the chance to hit golf balls with a PGA professional, but my friend has always been my friend first, and as a side issue, I am a preacher, and he is a golfer. I mention this because when you are living in the darkness of your heart, you don't need a lecture on providence, you need a friend who cares and loves you unconditionally. Bernhard set the mold that day of what it is to be called a friend. He is, to this day, one of my heroes, and I only fear that when we get to heaven, I shall not see very much of him. I am sure he will be so close to the throne of God, and I shall be so far back that I will only catch a glimpse of him. This is the same sentiment that was first shared by John Wesley about George Whitfield of the 1700's in England.

As the Parkinson's diagnosis was beginning to dominate my life I started to loose hope. The loosing of hope belongs to the dark side of life for when you lose hope you step into despair and despair leads to a sense of loss. We call it depression and it never strikes in an obvious way. It is normally disguised in an over concern and focus on our pain. We become engulfed with a pre-occupation of our life and we leave God at a distance. We are often told by well-meaning people to just believe and trust God. The truth is you cannot no matter how hard you try. God is not to be found. If you ever go through this dry moment in life you will know God has to strip us of our robe and pierce our very heart with his intentional love and grace before we can see the light of his grace. Only then, can we begin to live again with the anticipation of his hope in our life. It is the time of the meanwhile and that is why Genesis 37:36 is so strategic, so strengthening, and so shouldering for life. "*Meanwhile*, the Midianites sold Joseph in Egypt to Potiphar, one of Pharaoh's officials, the captain of the guard." Here within the "meanwhile" lies the rest of Joseph's story, my story... and perhaps yours.

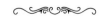

## The Darkened Chamber

My heart beats
With a fearful anticipation
That God's love no longer abides
And that his blessing has passed me by.

My life is not the same
As my purpose seems to wane,
The overwhelming loss
Of a future hope appear detained
As I sense the barrenness of his name.
The emotions of my soul
Are buried deep within
This earthen vessel of
Cemented clay that remains
Rigid, dried and indifferent
To trust again.
How shall I exist to
Feel, live, trust?
But just as I slip into
The dark chamber of a seared hope
The guardian of my life
Wedges open the chamber door
And begins to pour the aroma of his presence
Into the cracks of my hardened shell
And slowly, but in perfect time,
The softening kiss of his peace
Reminds me that he even lives
Within the darkest spot
And that he will not let me slip so deep
That I am forgotten
And that he is still molding the clay
Of which I have been made
So I may feel, live, and trust again
At the end of the day.

# The Meanwhile

There was something unique about growing up at 2402 Bernard Drive. We lived across the street from a Jewish synagogue. That was not the unique twist, even though it was the mid-1950s in a small North Carolina town. The parking lot at the synagogue provided a place for every kid to learn how to ride a bike on a smooth concrete pavement. For what seemed like weeks, but was only days, my mother would patiently take me over to the parking lot and carry on the thrilling but tedious task of teaching me how to ride a two-wheeler. The significant thing was that my mother, growing up in the Depression, did not know how to ride a bike because she never had one. But, be that as it may, she logically figured out the routine and gave me the basics. She would run alongside me, keeping pace with her one hand on the back of the seat of the bike. Every so often, I would get into my glide and yell, "I'm doing it! Riding on my own!" while balancing the bike against the pull of nature. At that moment, I would only be too quick to notice that my mother's hand would still be gripped on the back of the seat of the bike, balancing me and running full speed in order to keep up.

I am fifty-seven years old, married for twenty-eight years with three kids of my own. My mother is eighty-eight and far from being retired as she still works forty plus hours a week at a bank. She called me the other day to see how I was doing and, as every mother does, reminded me that I was not getting enough rest and asked if I was taking my vitamins. As I hung up the phone, I could not help but reflect back to a spring day at the Jewish synagogue where my mother informed me that one day I would ride that two-wheeler all by myself. That day has yet to come.

The providence of God, otherwise known as the never ending care of God, in our lives is much like my mother's hand on the back of the seat of the bike. He allows us to get into our stride, and at times, we are so bold to yell we are doing it all by ourselves, only to be reminded by a bump in the road that his hand is still there, guiding and controlling our lives. Solomon said it well in Proverbs 16:9 when he said, "In his heart, man plans his course, but the Lord determines his steps." Oh, I believe that God allows us to glide freely within the scope of his sovereign will. I have spent most of my ministry years in Florida, but if it had been North Carolina by preference, I believe I would still be in the will of God, and he would still be in control.

That is another chapter and perhaps another book, but for now, it is enough for me to say that not only is God omnipotent, but he also is omniscient;

he knows all. That means that in the living out of life, there are times, even seasons, which seemingly do not add up; moments that go against that hopeful view of life that every cloud has a silver lining and that there is always some disguised blessing to profit us.

Dream on, little brother Joseph, we might say. But the reality is that Joseph was on a caravan somewhere in the Hebron desert headed for the slave market of Egypt. This landed him in the home of a high ranking military leader under Pharaoh, which later proved to have its own challenges. Life was not bursting forth with a silver lining, some hidden treasure behind door number two. This was hell on Earth for this young teenager, and God was nowhere to be found. We may want to romance this part of Joseph's life and say how much he trusted God, kept up his devotional life with journaling, all the while singing, "Kumbaya, my Lord," but I believe this is far from the truth.

So then what is the truth? The truth is we are so afraid of being real and allowing ourselves to live within the tension of what we know of God and what we are experiencing in the moments of pain, failure, brokenness, and yes, even disillusionment. We don't like unanswered tension. We want the comfort of answers that will rescue us from pain and unsettledness and then we give some testimony someday about how we trusted God in the middle of the storm. Christian bookstores are filled with chronicles of how to live in victory and rise above the moment, but what I want to read and so long for as a pilgrim of Jesus is a testimony of just how to live.

Why are we so obligated to look for the blessing as if it will mysteriously appear only after we unmask it or just come up with enough faith for it to make its way into our lives? Now, don't get me wrong, I am not a fatalist, but I do think there are times when life stinks—and I mean really stinks. This, I believe, is a result of the fall of man in the garden.

What then do we learn about God from all this? It is a very practical but hard truth that there are times we hold on to God and wait…or better yet, he holds on to us. The fact is that God is never obligated to sing to us, "Just you wait and see, little sheep, Daddy's gonna buy you a golden ring. And if that golden ring doesn't shine, well then I'll give you something else to ease your pain." Trusting God and resting in his plan is when, in the heat of the moment, you are willing to live in the pain and know that he will not let you slip so deep that you are forgotten (even though for the time being you feel like a stepchild to God). Where is God in all this? He is right there with you, even though right now he is not tearing down walls at the sound of trumpets or appearing glorious in the desert within a burning bush. Right now, he is quiet and seemingly removed or indifferent. But as with Joseph, "meanwhile," God has a plan. And what a plan he has!

Living in the providence of God is living confidently that in the "while" of God's plan; life is sometimes just plain mean. That, my dear fellow journeyman, is trust. As my African-American preacher friends often ask, "Are you with me?" However, the real question is, "Is God with us?" If you are authentic enough to even ask that question, then you are ready to learn the lessons of the meanwhile and to live real in this world. If you are willing to live within the tension of God's sovereignty and man's will; well then, you have a story to tell that will be real and inspiring and will bring hope to hurting people.

In Proverbs, Solomon goes on to reveal the ways of man by stating, "A man's steps are directed by the Lord. How then can anyone understand his own way?" That, my friend, is honesty—when we can outwardly admit with Solomon the truth of his wisdom. Solomon says that God never intended for us to have it all figured out on the balance sheet of life. He never pretended to end the day as the benevolent grandfather in C. S. Lewis's book *The Problem of Pain*, who says at the end of the day that a good time was had by all. Contrary to what many of my evangelical friends believe, God's ultimate purpose for our lives is not to make us happy, purpose-driven people. His ultimate joy is to see us rest when we do not understand his purposes. That transfer of trust leads to supreme attention on God and that is God's prerogative—his jealousy for our attention. This is what we were created for. This is why Adam walked sheepishly in the garden after taking a self-motivated "bite" out of life. When he craved the satisfying juices of the exotic garden fruit, he chose to believe in that moment that God is motivated most of all when he sees his children dance by the light of the moon or stretched out on some sandy beach without a care in the world being waited on by the island butler. What Adam chose to believe that day was that God existed for man and not man for God.

This belief is noted well as we see the curse of the fall of man in Genesis 3:17–19: "Cursed is the ground because of you. Through painful toil you will eat of it all the days of your life—by the sweat of your brow, you will eat your food until you return to the ground; since from it you were taken, for dust you are and to dust you will return." God makes it very clear that man will seek to be independent, self-indulgent, and pursuant of his own needs to be satisfied. God, however, created man to be dependent on him for this noble existence, and therefore what he produced would bring glory to him and also man's contentment. The curse left man on his own and ultimately dissatisfied and empty. What Christ did on the cross was provide restoration so man may live within his created purpose, bringing glory to God.

The restoration of which I speak is no less than the process of sanctification—and that is exactly what it is, a process. You may not be experiencing victory today or perhaps have turned some corner in your walk with God that has spring boarded you into a deeper walk of faith, but if you are in Christ, then you are indeed in the process. I am not sure that God is so interested in how far we have gotten, for he knows that none of us get very far on any given day. If you think you are above the process, or better still, finished in the process, then check your pulse because you may be glorified. If that is the case, then you should cancel your plans for dinner because, to put it simply, you are dead. Oh yes, you're with

Jesus, but dead on Earth. The good news is that you will be able to listen in on a host of conversations that applaud how far others thought you got in the process, which of course will vary depending on their previous relationship with you. The process this side of heaven matters little as compared to the fact that you are in it. Now, am I saying that fruit does not matter, the fruit of a godly life? No, but I am saying that the volume of fruit is not the key, for that is the religion from which Christ sets us free! Counting fruit leads to legalism and manmade control, and legalism always ends in leaving one empty and defeated of joy. Pure sanctification happens when we begin to depend on God for even the air we breathe, not to mention our self worth. This is what God wants of us, our very selves yielded to him.

You say yes, but Paul promises that all things work for good in our lives which is proof that, in the end, even in the darkest time, he still has a blessing for us. Romans 8:28 has become one of those verses we love to quote in our consumeristic, evangelical world. We love it because we have conveniently misquoted it, but who is to argue about a little syntax mishap if it makes for good preaching? Just think about what we are saying. God indeed runs around, wringing his hands, trying to make sure that he does not even hear a whimper that we might be displeased, but if we are, he can assure us that in the end, we will be happy. So, try to keep it in your heart to trust him. This is not the God of the Bible; this is Madison Avenue. What Paul actually says is that we know that in all things God works for the good. And what is the good?

Paul says it is the purposes of God, not our latest spa experience—that even though hair removal is painful, the outcome is smooth skin. God's blessing is himself working for and in us. This is the silver lining, if indeed you must have one.

As I think about this biblical abuse, I shudder to consider how many times it must have been said to the families of the loved ones of the 9/11 victims in New York City in 2001. I can just hear it now from well-meaning Christians. "Cheer up because God has got a wonderful plan for your life. I know you're hurting and have been left alone to face life, but there is a silver lining, and it is just around the corner." That is not a lot of comfort to a young mother, staring life in the face with three kids, a mortgage, and all alone. Why won't we just let them grieve, ask a few hard questions as to why and come out on the other end as when Job said, "He knows the way that I take, and when he has tested me, I shall come forth as gold" (Job 23:10). Why? Because we are afraid we will not be able to give a neatly packaged and scripted answer. Living in the meanwhile means we are content to trust today when we are on a caravan to Egypt, and for the time, being things are not okay.

I learned that lesson hard with my son, Trevor. He was a high school golfer. He played on the varsity team and won a lot and lost a lot. One particular round, he was leading at even par after sixteen, but the last two holes, the wheels came off, and he double bogied seventeen and eighteen and lost the match. I approached him and quickly and got out my consoling words, "Its okay, Trevor," I said, hoping that would be enough to keep his lip from trembling. But my son looked at me and passionately said, "No, Dad, it's not okay." At that moment, my spiritual giant of a son crossed over into real maturity, recognizing that sometimes it is not okay, and yet God is still there. We want the blessing first before we can trust. We are like Tom Cruise in the movie *Jerry Maguire.* "Show me the money," as if God is now responsible to cough it up, the blessing that is. Whatever happened to just being quiet and waiting and perhaps never knowing the why? This is living in the meanwhile.

Joseph was on a caravan, and I have Parkinson's disease, and to be honest, I don't see a lot of good in all that. But I do see God who is in it, and I know he is good. Well-meaning believers have sought to comfort me by saying, "Oh, Pastor Mike, I can't tell you how blessed I am by your testimony and how you trust God." Many times I've wanted to respond, "Well, I am glad you think so and that you feel the blessing, but I would have been content by blessing you with a nice card." Living in the meanwhile is my call to simply rest in the knowledge that I don't need to *feel* the good; I only need to *know* that God is good in my life.

Now, please understand my heart. I'm not saying that God does not bless us or that he doesn't see the end of the story, which is always motivated by his glory and my good. God indeed blesses his children and joyfully so, but what bothers me is that we want to bypass the process of pain and get to the blessing. If we only see the blessing to be some climactic end, then we miss the blessing of the process. It was in the home of Potiphar that Joseph grew up and began to develop a reputation of leading, organizing, and implementing; lessons that would benefit anyone who would attempt to lead a nation during a national crisis that would last seven years. Joseph was developed by God within the experience of his pain, not at the end. That is the meanwhile.

One day, I made my routine three-month checkup to the neurologist. After going through the normal drill of tapping my toes, snapping my fingers, and walking up and down the hall as the doctor watched my arm swing, my neurologist asked me to sit down because he had a question to ask me.

"You know I am Jewish," he began.

"Yes," I said, wondering where he was going in this conversation.

"So tell me, what do I do about my sin?"

That's a loaded question for a preacher, and I began to share the freeing news of Christ. The conversation ended without an alter call or a signed decision card, yet God was working. I quickly made my way to the car and spoke to God in the midst of tears. "I've never told you this, God, and I had better say it now because I might not tomorrow. If having Parkinson's got me into that doctor's office and provided an opportunity for your message to reach a questioning life, then I thank you for the Parkinson's."

I've taken it back many times since, but what happened to me that afternoon was I became content living in the pain of stiffness and nervous gestures.

That is living in the meanwhile. I want to know why and how could it be good that at the age of forty-five, I was diagnosed with this disease. I want a walk in the sunshine and smooth sailing down the yellow brick road. In the front seat of my car, I came face-to-face with the fact that it is okay to not be, feel or act okay, but to wait as God indeed shows forth his glory. That is the process of the meanwhile. To be honest, I think that most of our lives are lived on the edge of the meanwhile. If not, then God remains removed and somewhat distant. Without the meanwhiles of life, we would simply check in with him every now and then, but with them, the meanwhiles, we realize that life is lived fully when we lean upon him for everything, because he *is* everything.

We have the end of the story with Joseph and yes, it is good. And because of that, we are able to trust him for the unknown ending of our meanwhile. Beyond our pain God is still God, and that alone makes it good. But will we always see the good, know the good, or feel the good? The answer is no! If we are willing to venture into that kind of unknown with God, then we are ready to learn the lessons of the meanwhile and find the depth of life that will truly have an impact for his glory. It is to this end that we were created. Living in the meanwhile means we are willing to live in the wondering of what God is doing because we are captivated by the wonder of who God is.

## Wondering

I wonder about a lot of things
That no answer seems to bring,
For I am told as the questions unfold
That in trusting I must cling.
I wonder why
There is hatred and strife
In a world that seems so filled with life.
I wonder why the day seems long
To those who seem to lose their song.
I wonder why there is little good
To those who search and long for food.
I wonder about a lot of things,
Little things, yet things so deep,
The questions over while I lose my sleep.
Why is it that the little man
Is often looked down upon in this Promised Land?
Why is it that men seldom cry?
Why is it the best seem to die?
Why is it that children who have no home
Only find comfort in the streets they roam?
And why is it that the guilty get by
Even though they refuse to comply
No answer seems to come forth strong,
Although in this my heart does long,
But I will trust the ruling throne
For in his counsel the answer is known.
So in this tension I will live
And wait upon his grace to give
The comfort needed in this age old quest
While we live simply as his earthly guest.

# Living with Guilt Unknown

Tucked almost silently between the pit and the palace of Joseph's life is the story of Judah and Tamar. Judah was, of course, the brother who did him in, and Tamar was Judah's daughter-in-law and the niece by marriage that Joseph, perhaps, never knew. The story is obscure and is most often overlooked. In telling the story, it is very clear that God's intent is to describe the subtle destruction of buried guilt and what it does in one's life when it is left unchecked and not allowed to surface. There is, however, a meanwhile in these dry times with God; as we will see with Judah and Tamar—a meanwhile that will show us the sure and careful grace of God.

Even in times of denial, God works a meanwhile, a meanwhile that goes beyond the story of Judah and Tamar and leads us right into the redemption of the world. The key is to keep this in mind as you walk through the events that followed, beginning the morning after Joseph was sold to the Ishmaelite caravan, now long on its way to Egypt.

Judah was the older, protective, yet passive brother. He had heard the dangers, seen the coat, and felt the father's obvious partiality to the favored son. Judah was the fourth son and the last birthed by Leah into this noble family. Reuben, Simeon, and Levi preceded, and at the birth of Judah, Leah determined to praise God—which indeed is somewhat prophetical of this line of redemptive history, for it all started in Genesis 29:31–35. The Bible says that at the birth of Judah, Rachel became jealous of her sister. At that moment, an intense family tension began, and it was in this environment that Judah was raised. He was always the reminder to Rachel of what she couldn't produce from the womb. In the course of ancient Eastern culture, Rachel was the resident stepmother, sort of a "mommy dearest" role model. Meal times must have been a strain for the happy clan of dysfunctional characters. Judah most likely never lived up to much of anyone's expectations. He was the youngest in the string of four, a curse to Rachel, and overlooked by his father. When Joseph was in that pit, it was Judah who, with his struggling ego, ambitiously said, "Let's sell him." This, of course, satisfied his need to be recognized, gain the respect of his brothers for his clever solution, maintain a sense of benevolence toward Joseph, and yes, make a little money on the side. Not bad for an underachiever. Judah got rid of his emotional competition without real blood on his hands. However, the guilt was worse than blood. This guilt would never be known to the father, or anyone outside the rat pack of plotting brothers for that matter. But no matter how much he suppressed his actions, his passive aggression toward his younger half-brother, he could not live with the failure that burned in his mind as he lay awake at night.

So no wonder chapter 38 begins, "At that time, Judah left his brothers and went down to stay with a man of Adullam named Hirah." Notice there is no mention of Jacob. In Judah's mind, there was nothing lost in leaving the man in whose eyes he had never measured up. But neither was there anything gained by a life of living with unsettled, hidden guilt, which indeed is the tragic story of Judah and Tamar. And it is at times the tragic story of our lives.

Let me take a moment for an important note. We are so far removed from Eastern culture that we struggle to understand the legitimacy of the family customs. We read the Old Testament with eyes of modern Western man, which violates a basic principle of hermeneutics (interpreting Scripture). Any serious Bible learner needs to realize that Scripture was written and granted by God, but within the chosen environment of an Eastern culture and geographical setting.

I recently moved away from Ft. Lauderdale, Florida. While there, I learned a vital lesson in managing the traffic customs. I truly think that when sitting at a stop light, there must be a color between the red and the green that cannot be seen but by a chosen few. In twelve years of residence, I never quite made the club. As the members of the "light club" sit at a traffic light, there is a secret color known only to them that appears somewhere between red and green, giving them permission to gun it ahead of all the nonmembers. If by some unfortunate twist of traffic providence the members get stuck behind a nonmember…well…they must wait one second longer. This, of course, ignites deep-seeded anger and the horn becomes a weapon of revenge, thus producing a culture of rudeness. All this to say: if I live in South Florida and expect to drive, I must either understand this unspoken rule or join the club. To be honest, I'm not sure how this fits into my explanation of Bible interpretation, but it makes for a good story and some comic relief in the middle of a heavy account of guilt. There is a point of legitimate application, however. Whether we are reading Scripture or driving in South Florida, we need to understand the customs of the land.

So when we come to the curious blend of family dynamics and cultural responsibility, we need not be shocked. Judah had three sons: Er, Onan, and Shelah. As with most names of the ancient world, these names had significance. In particular, it is worth mentioning that the Hebrew root of Shelah is *deception*. It doesn't take an ancient linguistic expert to figure out why God would allow such a name to appear on the redemptive chart. Deception was the curse of the fall and indeed the theme of Judah's life. Maybe we see here Judah's attempt to bring into the light his hidden guilt.

Now, I have two sons. I must admit that when my wife and I set out to pick boys' names, we had no agenda to create the atmosphere of their lives in their names. I know I am treading on sensitive ground here, but I had no desire to name my sons after one of the Minor Prophets, which seemed to be the real test of a spiritually tight home. We named them Trevor and Tyler because…well…we liked the names. Any mark they will make in life cannot be accredited to the meanings of their names.

Judah, on the other hand, had his conscience to deal with. For the life of me, I can't imagine sitting around with family and friends pointing out how cute "little Deception" is when he walks. Oh well. Call me shallow. But I do think it interesting that God is creating a redemption drama, one that is clouded by the deception of our sin. It is ironic that God chooses Judah to map out the lifeline of Christ. How great of God to include the off color, the seedy, those on the edge of life to represent his grace. This holds out a beckoned call to you and me—the mainstream, the normal…people who would name their sons Trevor and Tyler.

The deception of Judah, although unknown and unsettled, no doubt had negative effects on his family. The Bible says his oldest son, Er, was so wicked that God put him to death (Genesis 38:7), but before his tragic end, he married a woman named Tamar. We are not told how long marital bliss lasted for Er and Tamar, but it wasn't long enough to produce offspring (which in the ancient world normally happened within the first rendezvous of matrimony). This guy Er must have been some catch. But short into their marriage, Tamar was left a widow, happy, no doubt, to be single again. Singleness would be all too short lived for Tamar, as she was culturally forced to stay linked to this deceptive family. According to what was called the Levirate marriage custom (*levir* meaning brother-in-law), Tamar was given the wonderful opportunity to endure another Hollywood marriage with son number two, Onan, who, according to custom, was to lie with his brother's wife to produce offspring.

According to Deuteronomy 25:5–6, this obvious male-dominated law was given as a legal obligation within Israel. It takes on a romantic environment when illustrated by Boaz and Ruth, living out the kinsman redeemer call, but Tamar was simply caught in a web of sex in the city, Judean style. Onan, in true deceptive fashion, would spill his semen on the ground so as not to produce offspring for his beloved brother. The Bible says he did this because he knew the name-bearing children would not be his. Where did this guy come from? What should be obvious family loyalty is nowhere to be found as Onan was ruled by no evidence of love for his brother and maintained the family tradition of deception. God was none too pleased with this act of selfishness, and to show his displeasure, Onan was put to death by God, as well (Genesis 38:10).

At this point, if I were Shelah, Judah's third son, I would be thinking that the track record with this woman was not looking too promising, and if things took their natural course, I would be dead within a few short months, maybe sooner. But Shelah was spared this mental anguish for Judah also had this caution on his mind and told Tamar she would have to wait until his son was old enough to fulfill the responsibility of taking her as his wife. Judah, of course, had the perfect solution and told her to live as a widow until then in her father's house. By now, Tamar must have been thinking, *I didn't ask for this problem. I've been through two marriages with this family, and they both were trouble from day one. And their God killed off both of them. Now, why should I wait?* But wait she did, for a long time, until it was obvious she had been forgotten, and in keeping with Judah's reputation, deceived. At this point, we have the making of a drama that rivals anything you would see on the screen in Hollywood. God is on the move and always works behind the obvious. Remember this is a book about the meanwhile of life. In case you have forgotten, the meanwhile is when it doesn't appear God is making sense, but in reality, he is crafting out a plan that will reveal his work in and for our lives.

Before we go any further into this intense plot, it would do us well to ponder a moment on Tamar. She was experiencing a meanwhile of life. She had been used and deceived by Judah's family. She knew them to be religious, chosen people with historical heritage, matched by no other. They were the ultimate "first family," if you will, of Israel. So, what do you do when you know you are being deceived but you can't really prove it or even be believed? You bury it into the hidden crevices of your heart. So it appears that Tamar went home like a good little girl and seemingly faded away, out of sight, out of mind. Judah may have been hiding his guilt, but Tamar was plotting the revenge in light of his guilt. This time, Judah's deception would not escape notice. Though

Tamar may have been out of mind, she was, indeed, well in view.

The story continues to unfold with informants telling Tamar that Judah was on his way near her. His wife had died, and he was alone. Tamar was determined to punish her father-in-law, or perhaps she just wanted a baby out of all this unsettledness. In short, she appeared as a prostitute with a simple change of clothes. Into what? I doubt that she'd be stereotyped with a short skirt, high heels, and ruby red lipstick. For the life of me, I cannot figure out what is so alluring about this image, but if you go to almost any major city, you will find it displayed. Judah, in short, wanted to satisfy his male cravings. To put it honestly, he wanted sex, the nonattached way, and he'd be on his way. But one little detail would change his life and also begin to lay out the blueprint of God's story.

In biological terms, Tamar became pregnant. This would not have been any real concern to Judah, except he decided to leave behind his seal and cord, which, in modern terms, is his significance on a rope. Now if you were from the hood, the brothers no doubt would be wearing this as a fashion statement around their necks. This awkward drama concludes with it being revealed that the two boys to be delivered by Tamar were indeed to be the fourth and fifth sons of Judah; Perez and Zerah were their names. And at least for now, the deception is made accountable.

I am very much aware that what I have done in the preceding paragraphs is simply retell the biblical account of Judah and Tamar, but my attempt to bring the hidden into the light is to help us discover the meanwhile I believe to be so clearly taught.

Hidden, unaccounted for guilt can be so painful. Judah is a prime example that when we suppress our failure or just don't deal with our wickedness, we disrupt the very core of our lives. We often choose to simply move away, so we don't have to encounter those who know our little secrets (Genesis 38:1). Again, out of sight, out of mind. It is a plastic solution to this genuine condition of the heart. It is amazing to me that our cultures spends millions upon millions of dollars to look better, feel better, see better, smell better, and act better. We cure guilt by the simple purchase of the latest polo shirt (on sale of course) or the latest technology of television screens. But no matter how we cover the opening, the pit of guilt is still there.

There is a place on the Upper East Side of Manhattan named Perfect Tommy's, an after work bar for the young professionals. Out of a hectic work schedule and frustrated hurriedness, these young seekers developed a solution for their worried lives they called Velcro wall jumping. After a hard day, they suit up at Perfect Tommy's in a jumpsuit covered with Velcro, spring off of a small trampoline onto Velcro-covered walls, and score points like on a dart board. They note themselves as human bar flies and pride themselves with a host of emotions as they cheer on their colleagues. This, they say, is their outlet, their relief of stress, or better still, their cover-up of their inability to handle life in the mainstream. It catches the attention of the bizarre and will land them a spot on some talk show but will do very little to cure the hidden needs of their lives.

Yet, the truth is, we all have a Velcro-covered suit and some wall we use as a therapeutic solution to our needs. Some find it in a bottle, or some worn out syringe, or perhaps a more sophisticated way like an inscribed nameplate on an office door. No matter the attempt or the method, we seek to suppress some failure or need in our lives that, if known, would keep us from measuring up to the graven image of success.

Christians seem to approach this journey of significance in a much more subtle fashion. We choose to prostitute our devotion for God into a devotion of self-protection. We choose well-planned seminars and detailed notebooks of spiritual nuggets, copied from some orator, on life to help us feel better about ourselves. We have left our significance on a rope behind in some pit of need or failure that has left us feeling desperate about life. We know the hiddenness of who we really are will show up one day, but for now, we are content to coast on our efforts to move down into Canaan and hide. We are masters at suppression and novices at reality. The significance will show up one day, and ill-equipped as we are, we will pass it all off as none of us are perfect. Or we claim to live under grace, which we use as an excuse for sin rather than as an environment for growth, victory, and strength. Oh, there is grace, but only understood by those who understand the cost of victory.

Speaking of grace, look at how the story ends. But first, consider the meanwhile. We may be in the pit of hidden failure, grieving inwardly, wanting desperately for someone to find out and expose our need so we may be painfully yet completely freed up. The hiddenness develops a painful meanwhile and what we maintain as a false sense of comfort as all the while we are dying inside. We hear, "How are you brother?" and we respond with a false air of contentment, "Fine." All the while, we sense the meanness of a fallen world. Living in the meanwhile has become a cover-up for us—a reprieve for dealing with our need of brokenness. We seem to find ways to buy time from God by speaking the lies we learn in our cocoons. When the shock of our failed attempts to appear less than real has faded, we give some testimony to our small group of how we learned from our trial and how his strength is made perfect in our weakness. We don't know how to live real, because we never became vulnerable enough to learn and live real faith, a faith that is lived out noticeably on Main Street or at Perfect Tommy's or even before the neighbor next door. This faith starts with the meanwhiles of life when God appears silent as he did to Joseph, Judah, and yes, even Tamar. It is in the thick darkness of night where we learn to be sustained by the hope that morning will break us into the freshness of living again by God's unmerited grace which restores life, yet now more fully. But before we apply grace, we must develop and extend an atmosphere of grace.

This is where we come to the end of the story of Judah and Tamar. As obscure and curious as this story starts off, it ends with a direct casting role in the drama of God's redemption of mankind. The boys birthed by Tamar and fathered by Judah were named, as we have seen, Perez and Zerah. We are not told if Judah headed the household at any time. We are told that he never slept with Tamar again after the shock that bolted his life (Genesis 38:26). We are not told if there were weekend visits or if the boys realized that their grandfather was Jacob of Hebron. Their Hebron heritage, perhaps, bypassed their attention but did not escape their impact in the plan of God for sinners.

We have to leave Genesis and go to the small but redeeming book of Ruth to fully understand the impact of God's meanwhile in Judah and Tamar. Boaz and Ruth bore a son whose name was Obed, which means—in the Hebrew idiom—*servant*. This is a long way from the notion of deception represented in another son's name. You see, in Ruth, Obed was the father of Jesse, who, in turn, was the father of David. At this point, the book of Ruth embraces the total heritage of Obed and begins with the name of the head of the leading redemptive clan of Judah. The boy Perez grew up to be noted as head of the royal and redemptive people of Israel and Judah (Ruth 4:18–22). Perez started it all off as the father of Hezron, Ram, and Amminadab, and yes, a direct link to Jesse. He, in turn, fathered David, through whom the whole progress of redemption is seen in its earliest stages. Isn't it amazing that the unwanted and somewhat illegitimate son of Judah is listed in Ruth 4:18 as the head of the royal redemptive clan? This speaks volumes to me and should to all of us. In the meanwhile of failure and the testing moments of guilt unrevealed and unresolved, we are tempted to think we will never return to wholeness. We believe we did something to deserve the hardness of the moment, the loss, the struggle, and/or the pain.

After a summer of struggle in 2001, I entered the fall with a heaviness that dominated my mind and my feelings. I had spent a whole summer going from one doctor to another, trying my best to dismiss the Parkinson's diagnosis. I had spent countless hours talking to nutritionists, taking vitamins, and participating in holistic medicine cures, all to no avail to rid me of the ever-increasing stiffness. One afternoon, I was with a close friend. He said in his determined manner, "It is time to get to the bottom of this, and I'm sending you to the Mayo Clinic in Rochester, Minnesota. My doctor will see you and will determine once and for all what is wrong."

I couldn't deny that I needed his solution or that deep down I wanted to settle the questions I had and the condition I was trying to escape. So off Linda and I went to Rochester. In the impending days, the moment came to sit before the head of the neurology department and hear his results. Calmly and yet compassionately, he confirmed what the Duke Doctors had told me in June. It indeed was early onset Parkinson's. After a brief discussion of optimism for future treatment, Linda and I had dinner and returned to our hotel room.

In the middle of the night, I awoke to the fear that I must have done something wrong; some buried, unsettled sin had caused all this and now

God was making me pay up. I wept that night out of fear—a fear that took root in my mind and soul and would prove to hinder my joy and cripple my personality for months to come. I fell that night into the pit of despair. And as I saw it, there was no way out. I was now trapped within a broken body. The depression of emotion can strike hard and invade our ability to see beyond the moment. All I could see was abandonment by God because he appeared silent and harsh. Just like the apparent displeasure with Judah and Tamar, God knew something about me that would remain, perhaps, even unknown to myself. The weakness I began to experience was real, confusing, and left me wondering if God had given up on me. I wrestled with God on the basis of "why me" rather than "why not me," forgetting that he owes me nothing. I had once again forgotten grace, and I had kept myself from the fruit that God was still on the move in my life. Even if I had guilt unknown, my life was still to be filtered through the unconditional love of God. For like the line of redemption, there was always room for one more Judah or Tamar, or better still, a Perez.

The meanwhile of believed failure and thus deserving of the harshness of God would lead me into the temptation of self-centeredness, worry, and removing myself from almost everybody, including my family. The pulpit I had filled for almost ten years was emptied of my presence and never again experienced the casting of my shadow upon its stage. The terrifying thought that I was guilty, thus deserving Parkinson's, would lead me down a path of lostness. My heart was numb to grace, and no matter how hard I tried, I could not move into the joy of the dawn. It would be weeks later that I would be awakened to my first encounter with the true, freeing, and healing grace of God, which would reveal the joy of the morning and begin to restore my life. Restoration indeed would come and recovery from depression would be given, but not before the sting of defeat.

Judah left his brothers and went down into Canaan to bury his guilt. We are left with a story of redemption the hard way. Life sometimes is mean because we live in a mean world, fallen from the glory of God. But if we learn to rest in these times of God, then we learn a valuable lesson of the meanwhile of life, and that is that no matter how deep we sleep in our fallen nature, we still can be awakened to the awaiting grace God provides by his divine initiative.

In the following weeks, as I seemed more and more removed by the depression, I began to experience closeness and a realness of God that I had never quite understood. God was taking the initiative in my life, and during the meanwhile of his apparent silence and my false sense of guilt, God was preparing me for the explosion in my life that would prove to be more mentally destructive than my physical condition had ever threatened. It was at this point I began to comprehend more deeply God's awaiting grace that would allow me now to know what it was to touch the hem of his garments and conquer the temptations of defeat that would invade my life at home and threaten the very foundations upon which I had lived.

So I ask you, what is this bizarre and dramatic story doing in the midst of Joseph's story? Perhaps, God is showing how sin will catch up with you, even if you thought you had hidden it. Perhaps he is warning us that sin is always more costly to our lives than we can ever imagine. These are worthy answers to the reasons for Judah and Tamar. But think with me for a moment. I believe God is showing that even in our failure—hidden or unhidden—God is still at work in our lives. The redemptive plan of God is carried out by those who did not provide a good beginning. Judah and Tamar had their own issues, but together, they showed us the need is always there in our lives. Tamar is one of three women mentioned in the genealogical records of Jesus, thus establishing her link to Israel's royal history. Imagine the scared, bitter, and lost young woman who birthed the hope of grace. If you're living in the midst of failure and God seems removed and indifferent, then hold on to the meanwhile of God because it is about to get exciting...intensely hard, but exciting.

# This Pain

This pain, Lord, is deep inside,
Although my body aches
As I cannot move,
And my hand, I cannot hide.
The day will come,

I sense it not too far,
When my body becomes so hard
And I am left to live within your guard.
But allow me to still squeeze the side
Of the one who has stood with me
Within this tide.
It grieves me, Lord,
To a point of probing despair
As I realize before
Others I no longer compare
Within the eyes of the
Ones who held such pride.
They think I can do more
But no one knows
The pain within my door.
So as I journey home,
I pray in failure I will not roam.
And please, Lord, let me believe
That strength will return to me.
For this is my greatest pain
As I walk upon this lane.
So let me get home before dark,
So my joy is not left without a spark.
It is your peace that keeps me still,
As I am engaged within this lonely hill.
For the reality of this pain
Has now decided to remain.

# The Meanwhile of
# Never-Ending Temptation

So there he was, on a caravan to Egypt, stripped of his robe, and emptied of his self-dignity. Joseph now wore a borrowed garment, and all he had left were memories of the Hebron hillside and, of course, his dreams. I wonder how many times he must have sat and regretted he ever shared his dreams, wishing he'd just kept quiet. I am a very open person, but sometimes you can be too open. And if you are, you must be willing to face the consequences.

In that vein, consequences had arrived at Joseph's door. The consequences would land him a spot in the plush surroundings of a very influential man and his seductive bride (who goes unnamed). Joseph was seventeen, and this roller coaster of experience would make him aggressive and, for the first time, would lead him down a path of responsibility. This indeed was a good thing, but how do you tell a seventeen-year-old that making him suffer will lead him to paradise? Frankly, the pit that had been dug for him must have seemed removed when the man Potiphar put down the money to pay for his ownership of

Joseph. However, bought or sold, Joseph was on his way to a rich man's house. There would be no more borrowed clothes for this boy, for he was used to the finer things. I can imagine when he made it to his room; he must have stretched out on his bed with hands folded behind his head and thought, *Things could be worse. I mean, I miss my family, but once a prince, always a prince.* He must have fallen asleep that first night with a sense of sweet revenge. *One day, they will regret this.* But little did he know then that this was just another step on the road to brokenness in order for God to shape him.

That brings up an interesting question: does everything happen for a purpose? Oh we say it does and even in the world of hardness of heart, the thought is expressed, "It happened for a reason." Most of the time, we reason with comfort that the "reason" is always something good, never wanting to admit those hurtful, even seemingly unfair moments in life can always be part of God's "reason" in our lives.

God was out to shape Joseph in such a way that would challenge to the utmost the fibers of his natural hormones. Joseph was seventeen, and Genesis 39:7 says he was "well built and handsome." If living today, he would likely be working for Abercrombie and Fitch or some other label of recognition. The story unfolds by saying that "his master's wife took notice of Joseph." Wow, is this not an understatement? To put it in common language, she had the hots for this young man—a modern day cougar. Day after day, she would present her advancements, and day after day, Joseph would refuse. The significant thing about this story is that this confrontation with Potiphar's wife was not just a momentary experience. This would continue for eleven years. How do we know that, one might ask? It's a simple mathematical conclusion. Joseph was sold at seventeen and entered into Potiphar's house. He was sent into Pharaoh's service at the age of thirty, according to Genesis 41:46. That's thirteen years. Since he spent two years in prison, that means he was twenty-eight when he entered prison. Therefore, we can safely conclude that the previous eleven years were spent in Potiphar's house with daily sexual advances from Potiphar's wife (Genesis 39:10). Now, do you see the impact of his victory? Joseph was at the peak of his dating years. He was young, handsome, single, and all alone in a foreign land where nobody knew or cared. He was raised by a Hebrew with Jehovah God. Nobody would have ever known if just once he would have satisfied his bouncing hormones and caved into having sex with this perhaps rich, beautiful, maybe older woman. Nobody would have even held him accountable. And on the local scene, no one would have thought it to be unusual. Joseph could have thought, *I deserve a little fun, a little quick fling, a brief rendezvous with passion.*

But integrity had something to do with it all— integrity toward the God who was there in his life and the earthly master he had pledged to work for and honor. *Can I do such a wicked thing and sin against God*, he would ask, however never expecting any answer or support from those around him. The account says that he refused to go to bed with her and also even to be with her (Genesis 39:9–12). This is astounding, and in a moment, we will see a point of application. But for now, we must see the rest of the story. Potiphar's wife would not take no for an answer, and finally, one day, she cornered him, having planned a day off for her household servants—either that or they all responded to a sudden fire drill that took them all outside. So this time, sexually aggressive, she caught his cloak and pulled him to her bedroom. Every fiber in his blood-pumped muscular body must have told him to go for it. If not, then she must have been some kind of ugly. The fact is, he refused again, but the only way out this time was to run, and run he did, leaving her tightly held embrace. This is so vivid, for he managed to pull away but left his coat behind, a coat recognizable to be his. Joseph had a thing for coats, and once again, God has to use a coat to begin to break him. For the second time, a coat gets him into trouble with man yet broken before God.

Potiphar's wife's pride was wounded, and to save face, she accused him of attempted rape, when in fact she had attempted to rape him. The story continues to unfold down a different path of learning for Joseph. We will explore that later, but for now, what do we see that will help us in our meanwhile moments of sustained, perhaps sudden, or maybe just momentary temptation? How do we withstand the continual advances of the world? How do we live pure when every pull of our human person is telling us to live free of biblical restraints, whether from sexual activity or overdosing on chocolate ice cream, causing our thirty-two-inch waist to grow to a thirty-six because of our lack of discipline? Oh, I know Christians in America would challenge the validity of calling the latter a sin, but according to the Bible, it is just as much a sin as the attempted sex from Potiphar's wife. Can you imagine a Christian bookstore owner putting front and center a book on the fallen life of financial mismanagement next to a book on the curse of homosexuality as if they were equal? We have become so desensitized to sin. Most wonder why we don't just let up on Joseph. Let him have his little fling and then repent. If anything, it will land him a book deal on how to fight sexual failure now that he has fallen and knows how it really is. Isn't that how it works? No wonder there is little difference between teenagers of the world and the church. "Not my little Johnny," you say. Well, let me tell you, your little Johnny might be having his devotions every night, but there is a great chance that he has also had a midnight snack from the world; God forbid that we be so honest and so real with ourselves.

That is why Joseph stands out. From him, we can learn four truths. The raw truth is that the following will not protect our lives from the world but will direct us from the world's grip.

The first key to un-gripping the world is *humility of self*. At every point, Joseph refused self-gratification. He asked in a moment of debate, "How can I do such a wicked thing and sin against God?" He again; initiated his will in Genesis 39:10 when the Bible says, "He refused to go to bed with her." Here we see a powerful lesson of personal courage and discipline. By now, perhaps somewhere in his early to mid-twenties, Joseph was living out the truth that God did not owe him in life, and neither did anybody else. He was not blinded by an attitude that he was due for God to throw him a bone and say, "Good boy." His question indicates that he saw himself as one who owed God rather than as the one to whom God desired to do anything just to make him happy. Humility ruled the day, and Joseph was left coatless. He then stood at the local hangout trying to explain why he was not wearing all his clothes. Have you ever wondered where Joseph went when he ran off? Did he hide? Or was this a case of the emperor is wearing no clothes? Joseph denied the passion normal to every man on this planet. Joseph was living by the code that life was not about him but about the glory of God. This is the first step of brokenness.

I remember my first role as a senior pastor. Somewhat newly married for only two and a half years, we had just had our first child, a son. I was called by God (plus the fact that I wanted to return to the land of creamed corn and sweet iced tea) to a church in South Carolina. They said they were broken and that they needed me. (At the time, this was an ego boost, but years later, I found out that I was the only one who didn't turn them down.) At thirty-two, I was up for the challenge and believed that I could do anything. I am not sure when it all started, but the fact that deep down I saw myself as next in line after Billy Graham might be a tip off to my need to first be broken. Things were going well, but I hit a wall. The fact is, I was into the image rather than the image maker. After a sizeable growth, the summer months hit the church, and one Sunday in June of 1988, the attendance was lower than when I first came. I was devastated, for we all know that the sign of spiritual blessing is bigger numbers week by week. I went home, felt sorry for myself, cried, and told God what a mistake he had made. I imagine at this point God was chanting, "Yadda, yadda, yadda" and saying to himself, "The next thing he will say is that now I don't have a replacement for Billy Graham if I ever need one." Then God spoke to me. No it wasn't audible, but it was real enough to me. "Michael, this is not your church, it is mine. And, if I want to grow it, I will. And, if I want to take it down to a storefront, then I can do that as well. And, by the way, I do have a replacement for Billy Graham, and it is not you." That pivotal moment proved to be foundational bedrock for the rest of my life. Dying to self may take on a variety of different approaches. It may be voluntary or forced, and it may be relatively pain-free or an absolutely heart-wrenching loss. But the common thread in all these expressions is our turning from self-sufficiency to God-dependency and contentment about it all.

The second principle to un-gripping the world from our lives is *the honor of God and his holiness*. Notice again Genesis 39:9, "How then could I do such a wicked thing and sin against God?" Joseph's concern was not self-pleasure. What a chance for Joseph—sort of an ancient preview to the movie *The Graduate*, silk stockings and all. What changed the course of events was Joseph's delight in God over his hormones. God was prevalent and personally affected by his actions. It was godliness that would rule the day because God was ruling Joseph's soul.

It was some months after my departure from the church as senior pastor that the depression seemed to get worse. I continued to feel lost and misplaced. Everyday, I allowed myself to feel as though I had been overlooked by God. I questioned everything about myself and God. I wasn't ready to be shelved by God, but it seemed I had been. And, for what reason? People would compliment my apparent faith of positivity, but it really was my pride, not wanting to be seen as weak. They would say, "Oh, what a blessing," and I would think, "Go read a good book. I don't want to be the poster boy of freedom and pain." I was anything but free. I was held tight by the world's grip of "protect self and smile while you're doing it." In my mind, I was quoting Philippians 4:13, "I can do all things through Christ who strengthens me," with an emphasis on *I can*. This kept those who believed in me convinced that I was still somebody, and it kept me in control.

One early morning, unknown to me, my wife had called one of the associate pastors I had worked with who also served as the counselor on staff along with another counselor who was a personal friend. Linda had been up all night with me and frankly had had enough. If I didn't get help and get away or change, she was going to have to leave for a while to keep her head together and our family in gear. In the backroom, they determined that I needed to go to a hospital. Yes, *that* kind. Only out of desperation, I consented. *Plus*, I thought, *maybe they will just knock me out, and I won't have to face the day.* They lured me with the description that it was the Cadillac version. I would have my own room and chocolates on my pillow each night, a kind of spa for the emotionally hurting. After all, it had a Palm Beach address. I don't know what happened to the place between the time of their pledges and my arrival, but this was not Camelot for the confused. It was jail for the jarred in life. There was no private room, and I had to turn in my razor every morning to my attendant as if having it threatened my life and maybe others. Was this really for me? I gave in to the fact that it must be, but those who brought me felt my pain and sensed this was the wrong place. I was indeed in need of help, but learning to play checkers during recreation time was not quite what I had hoped for.

We slipped away only to go to another one across the state. Upon my entrance, I learned they had me mixed up with another man by the same name, a lawyer in Miami who was coming for alcoholism. We left. That night, I was glad for my own bed. I felt I had dodged a close one, but this was the preface to a long-awaited surrender to the control and honor of God. It would be months later that I lay stretched out over my bed alone before God and with longing passion cried out, "God what do you want me to do?" At that moment, without hesitation, God spoke. Yes, spoke. I don't feel the need to qualify it for those who are blindly uncomfortable with the notion that God spoke. My best advice is, get over it. He speaks. He has never stopped speaking to the souls who will seek him. I am not sure what theological boundaries this breaks or doctrinal camps it disrupts, but he, God, spoke to me, and I listened for the first time in a long time. What he told me that day was in the vein of Naman and Elijah in Second Kings 5—unusual, unexpected, and unlikely. You remember, or maybe you're honest and don't. Nevertheless, Naman was told to wash seven times in the river and his leprosy would be gone. Now, God didn't ask me the same, although I was living in a home with a pool.

I asked, like Vivian Leigh in *Gone with the Wind*, "What shall I do?"

He said, "Stop taking your medication…all of it."

My response was more blunt than Naman's to Elijah's servant. I simply said, "I can't do that." It was said with respect but determination.

God responded, "I am God, and will you trust me?"

It was a heavenly, "Pardon me? You said what? Do you care to repeat that?" His rebuke led to my surrender to his honor. He was God, and I would trust Him. That was the bottom line. The results of that rendezvous with my Redeemer would come, but at that moment, I saw and stepped into his honor; his rule of holiness. And that was the un-gripping gesture of the spirit of God to put me on a path of holiness.

I express these moments of my life because when temptation overcomes us, it is because we lose sight of God's honor. Joseph determined he could not do that because God was God, and the honor of God had spoken. If you are gripped by the world and headed for the bottom of a reeking pit, then stop dead in your steps and listen and surrender to his control. If you are bold enough to ask, "What do you want me to do?" then be ready for him to bring forth the unexpected solution. And if he tells you to wash seven times in the river, then for Christ's sake, his glory's sake, wash, my friend. If you are in the unsolvable defeat of your life, then God is on the verge of astounding you with his power and honor.

The third principle logically follows, for when we see his honor; we will understandably sense *the heaviness of sin.* Joseph said in retort, "How could I do such a wicked thing?" He was definitive about what sin is. Notice he did not say, "How could I make such a mistake?" or "How could I be so dysfunctional?" No, he called the temptation wicked. He was sensitive to sin.

Today, we have been duped into thinking that our environment sets us up for sin, and indeed any failure we have incurred is certainly explainable by some psychological profile of how we were raised. Joseph, on the other hand, did not have that luxury. Sin was wicked, period. The bluntness poses a problem for many today. We want instant gratification, not an admission to sin. What we need in this cultural environment today is repentance—hardcore, honest lifestyles of repentance. We don't need conferences or seven-step programs to freedom. We don't need orchestrated events that stage repentance where we say, "Been there, done that." I recently was almost amused yet angered at a well-known speaker who was traveling the country, promoting an event he was hosting, ticketed only, so that people would come and repent. Oh, God, what are we doing? Repentance is now event-manufactured, with music and all. And I bet there could be T-shirts available, saying, "I repented, did you?" or something like that. Or maybe, "I went to the repentance fair, and all I got was this lousy T-shirt." I thought the reformation put an end to all this. Where are the Martin Luthers of today? Whatever happened to individual remorse where you settle it with God alone and come away with a clean life? It would be the mainstream if we only knew the heaviness of sin in the face of the holiness of God.

The fourth and final un-gripping movement of God is *the hardness of brokenness.* Joseph was put in prison; a prison that most likely made the pit in the desert some eleven years earlier look like the luxury suite at the Hilton. This could not be happening again, but it did. At the bottom again, with seemingly no way out.

I won't linger long here, for this whole book is about living on the edge of brokenness. I will simply conclude that seeing ourselves as inadequate to host the victory of God without his direct presence and power is the fertile ground in which brokenness takes place and restoration is birthed. If God is taking you down to your underwear, then move over Calvin Klein, God is ready to remold your life into an Adonis of hope. The meanwhile of God is always at work.

I can't move away from this topic without mentioning Genesis 39:20–21, "But while Joseph was there in the prison, the Lord was with him. He showed him kindness and granted him favor in the eyes of the prison warden." Here it is: the meanwhile. Even repentant, damaging, and controlling temptation can be the stage for the meanwhile of God in our lives. Unlike Joseph, we may be living in defeat, worn out by repeated failure, or just tired of trying to stay strong. We have lost hope and given into the notion that this is just the way life is for us. Whatever the condition of your drama, God is in the making of a meanwhile. There is no event to celebrate it or call for it. Lights, camera, video turned off, and the stage cleared. It is just you and God. What will it be? Grace is never more prevalent than when our failure or our temptation is most noticeable. This is not justification for sinful behavior but allows us to live within the boundary lines of the grace of God. God may still reveal his glory in our weakness. This is the good in the meanwhile of our defeat. For most of us, the meanwhile is just an experience away.

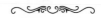

## Failure's Journey

Failure echoes a disturbing voice,
Ushered in by a forbidden choice.
It speaks the words familiar to all,
Expressed in the moments when we fall.
It has no preference between night and day
And leaves the life tainted and betrayed.

The conscience is seared
When God is not revered,
And a sense of shame
Challenges the power of his name.
Now as failure seems to chase
Those whom it would embrace,
The soul is tested deep
To awake from spiritual sleep
And therefore opens wide to realize
The danger of its compromise.
So as we pilgrim home
While in failure we have roamed,
Remember it is his name we bear
As we face failure's scare.
May we look to heaven's face
So our lives will know his grace,
And as we seek to share
In the victory that appears so rare,
Let it be said,
Not our will, but his instead.

# The Meanwhile of Being Forgotten

It was a cold December morning in 1968 when I first remember being forgotten. My father's career had moved us to Pittsburgh, Pennsylvania. On that Sunday morning, I waited expectantly by the door for my ride to church. The elderly couple next door had made me sort of their surrogate grandson and seen to it I attended the Allison Park Presbyterian Church. Pop Stewart would proudly march me down with him to his normal pew where I would sit and take in the teaching of the day. I was never particularly moved by this stoic experience, but he always seemed pleased I was there. Out of bitterness toward God, his wife had stopped attending with him shortly after the death of their youngest son. The tension was always obvious.

But this Sunday morning was different. He forgot me. He just went by himself and left me waiting. Even from the age of thirteen, I remember that feeling that left me empty and alone. I couldn't understand why he just forgot me and didn't seem to regret it. I felt abandoned and unimportant from this grandfather image in my life. But God had a meanwhile in play far beyond me that would be reached within hours. The meanwhile would prove to be life-changing.

Now picture this: Joseph was miles away from home. He was happy living the vida loca in Potiphar's house…but with limits. Today, we would spiritually wordsmith it and call it spiritual values and convictions. In fact, today, we would expect Joseph to create a teaching seminar on purity—T-shirts and all, quipping, "I ran. You can." Instead we find him back in the pit; except this time, the pit is an Egyptian prison. It is like hearing the phrase, "Cheer up, things could be worse." So we do. And sure enough, things get worse. I mean really, hadn't Joseph had enough? Then he was kicked again, and this time in the gut. So what did he do? Once again, he rose to the top of his class. The once favored son who became the favored servant in a rich man's house was now the favored prisoner. Oh come on! This is getting a little thick for human consumption. Besides being the warden's little angel, he took up dream interpretation in the prison. This is a twist. Not only did he have dreams himself, he went on to tell others what their dreams meant. This was a long shot for a young guy whose present reality went against his youthful dreams of superiority and rule. Things did not look promising for he was a long way from ruling. He was in the bottom of a third world prison, and this boy was not going anywhere any time soon. We are not told how long it took; save the phrase "some time" (Genesis 40:4). These words seem to indicate a considerable amount of time before Joseph became proven in his character. He was made a sort of personal valet to two highly visible political prisoners—the chief cupbearer and the chief baker. If you wanted to get close to the ruling family, these were the men to know. But somewhere along the way, they had fallen out of favor with the ruling class, yet not out of notice. The two men had dreams the same night and both awoke depressed and dejected; it was quite noticeable. Enter Joseph with a question of almost a smart-aleck tone. "Why are your faces so sad?" Now just think. You're sitting there in a prison, having had tasted the good life, and this kid asks you, "What are you so upset about?" Your first reaction is you want to punch him. They, however, left their aggravation behind and saw this nuisance of a kid as beneficial to their cause of getting out of prison.

Joseph was not cavalier about his talent. He saw the circumstances of his life, the meanwhile if you will, as opportunity for feasting on the glory of God. They were sad about a lack of answers to their dreams, and he was glad to say, "Look what God can do." Put it on pause for a minute. This, my friend, is the stage for the meanwhiles of our lives. No matter what they are about or who they are for, we sometimes are saddened by the setbacks of life, but we can, for at least a moment, see the gladness of showing forth what God can do. We sang it so freely as kids: "Jesus loves me, this I know, for the Bible tells me so. Little ones to Him belong. They are weak but He is strong. Yes, Jesus loves me." And so on. You remember. There is a childlike faith in trusting God in the meanwhile of discomfort and, in Joseph's case of being forgotten, not remembered. There is childlike faith in saying, "I can't, but God can." The pause button is on in our lives, and we want to remind God that one day we were or had been important to some circle of self-generated greatness. We are no longer in the game, and we wonder how this could be good. Joseph said, "Do not interpretations belong to the Lord?" (Genesis 40:8). With no self-glory, Joseph was only living in the midst of God's agenda. So with anticipation he said, "Tell me your dreams." They did, and the rest of the account is memorable to even the most novices of biblical minds. Joseph began with the cupbearer; a sort of personal wine taster or the secret service of vineyard delights. Ultimately, his dream predicted his release, and so you can imagine the anticipation in the chief baker's mind when he said, "I too had a dream." Joseph responded in verse 19 by saying, "Within three days, Pharaoh will lift off your head and impale your body on a pole. And the birds will eat away your flesh." Now, if I was the chief baker, I would ask Joseph to think again and then regret that I had ever even asked.

Here is another pause button. How many times do we sincerely want God to answer, to show us his will, and then when he stares us in the face with an answer, it is not to our desire? We say, "Look again," as if God has a crystal ball and is communicating his will at some country fair while guessing the weight of the fat lady. Our obedience at this moment is crucial because it is an act of our will that says we die to self and seek God above all else. It is the attitude of God. How many of us need to just tell God, "I had a dream too," and wait for his plan to unfold?

Well, the dreams were answered just as Joseph said which I imagine increased his reputation. But (there always seems to be a "but"), the book of Genesis says in verse 23, "The chief cup bearer, however, did not remember Joseph; he forgot him." At this point, our emotions are stirred because we have all been forgotten at some point in life. And if you have not, then cheer up, you will be. So what are the lessons of this pause button or meanwhile in our lives? The thought of being forgotten is so foreign to our human makeup. Graduation speeches never end with a statement like, "Go into the world and be forgotten." No. Everything we are influenced by suggests the opposite. Go into the world and make a name for yourselves. Leave a legacy and pioneer your dreams.

I must admit to you that that is the last thing I want to hear when I feel left out, left alone, and leftover. The reality is there are moments in life we will feel used up. We know God is writing an intense play of his glory, but we just wish we were not the main characters. We spend most of our lives seeking to be remembered and live for the moment to return to our high school reunions and have people talk about our winning touchdown, our starring role in the school play, or our magnificent speech in the debate club. Instead, they're talking about, under their breaths, how glad they are they married someone else, or how we were the last one they expected to turn out so…well…normal.

Let's face it. People have short memories when it comes to affirming others, showing thankfulness, or remembering the good points within a moment of failure. We have all been there—the point when all the work you've done has been looked over and someone else gets the promotion or your territory is cut back and not someone else's. We all remember the person who didn't show up when we were hurting or the person who didn't stand with us in the moment of debating our point. We have all been the offended and the offender.

In this case, Joseph was the offended. The Bible says Joseph was forgotten by his would-be redeemer, the cup bearer. This was not just for a moment but for two years. Can you imagine the increasing disillusionment in Joseph's heart? He had made a verbal condition with the cup bearer, "Remember me…to Pharaoh, and get me out of this prison" (Genesis 40:14). I am certain there was no ill intent meant by the cup bearer. Perhaps, he would awake at night thinking and saying to his wife Rhoda (there is always a Rhoda in the story), "Remind me to tell Pharaoh about the dream boy I met in prison." Well, maybe not, but there does not seem to be any justification for his forgetfulness of Joseph. He just forgot.

There are times in life when we are the targets of others' failures. We get hurt by their intended or unintended actions. Sometimes, we choose to embellish the hurt and build walls, cut off communication, refuse to show up at the family reunion, and remind others of our burden. Our good Christian friends respond by holding out some spiritual jargon such as, "If they persecuted Jesus, they will persecute you," or the real heart-wrenching one, "Just think how Jesus felt on the cross." This, of course, just adds to our hurt because, now, nobody understands how we feel, and we are left alone in the sea of self-pity.

One thing I have learned from moments like this is that most of the time, they are all caused by an out of balance view of my self-importance. The old-fashioned word is pride. There is one thing about Joseph that you will see repeatedly: he remained silent. He didn't demand to be heard and whine to the prison administration that his rights had been violated. He didn't cast shadows on his offender, reminding all how ungrateful the cup bearer was. He just kept quiet. And by keeping quiet, he was able to see God and to wait for the meanwhile of God.

Now you might say, "Yes, that's all good. But deep down you know how bad it feels to be forgotten after all I have done." There it is. The "I" neatly packaged in self-justification. Somehow in the "all we do" part of it all, we seek to define ourselves. When we are rejected, forgotten, and overlooked, we are devalued not only in our own eyes but also, we think, in the eyes of others. It is at this moment we define who we have sought to live for. We say we have been living for others and ultimately God, but the truth is, we have lived for ourselves and that is the problem. We wish God would allow a moment in our lives where, after we think we are okay with not being like him, we could hear Him say, "I'm sorry. Daddy didn't mean to hurt you. Let's do it again, and this time I won't be so insensitive to your hurt." If he did, he would no longer be God, but he would be our personal genie in a bottle. We would miss the meanwhile of his plan and thus, miss the fruit of real value before him.

Now back to Joseph…well there he was waiting for his emancipation from prison. Soon, he would trade prison shackles for more comfortable surroundings; perhaps, the cup bearer had a spot for him in Pharaoh's court. Each morning, as he would hear the shuffling footsteps of the prison guards, he would anxiously think, "Today is the day I am set free," and each morning he would be reminded of his plight by the deafening sound of the cell doors once again, closing shut.

Then the morning came after two full years. Isn't it interesting that God does nothing fast in Joseph's life, or does he in ours? God is not bound by man's concept of time. We have an agenda for our lives, but God brews his will over time as he produces the real motivation behind his actions. Yes, this is the meanwhile. I live there on the edge, and so do you.

Pharaoh had two dreams that unsettled him to the point that he sought answers as to their meaning. His advisors could not give him an understanding to the dreams. They most likely attributed them to the food he had eaten the night before. If you have ever eaten mid-Eastern food, then you know. In the midst of their confusion, the chief cup bearer said to Pharaoh, "Today I am reminded of my shortcomings" (Genesis 41:9). In other words, where has my mind been these past two years? This is classic self-protection. He thought that if he reminded Pharaoh of the time that he was the object of Pharaoh's anger, then something else might trigger Pharaoh's wrathful emotions, and he would be back in prison. Those were years, we imagine, he wanted to forget. You can almost feel his reluctance as he mentions Joseph to Pharaoh and then Pharaoh sends for him. Another routine morning for Joseph, but this morning was different. The meanwhile was beginning to be played out.

Joseph's response was powerful. It was physical and it was emotional. Notice his actions as verse 14 tells us, "He shaved and changed his clothes." Here is a simple thought. Joseph prepared himself to be in the way of blessing. The musty smell of the prison floor must have had an overpowering smell that permeated his clothes and skin. So, he took a bath. I don't want to over spiritualize the fact that Joseph prepared himself for the moment. Buried deep in those actions is a principle for life. Keep yourself ready to have God show you the meanwhile. Take steps to put your life in the way of God's truth and holiness so that nothing hinders your journey. The writer of Hebrews put it this way: "Lay aside the sin that so easily besets us and fix your eyes on Jesus." There are times when we need to shave and bathe in the midst of our meanwhile so we may notice what God is doing.

But Joseph's attitude of himself, and foremost God, is vital to see at this time. If it were you or me, the first thing most of us would have done is file a class action civil law suit against the government. We would make sure the cup bearer got a piece of our mind and that Pharaoh realized what a mistake it had been to keep our attributes hidden for two long years. *They will hear from me*, we would have thought. Why is it that we dream of the moment to tell the ones in our lives how much they hurt us or how insensitive their action was? "I just have to be honest," you say. No, you just have to remain silent, or more pointedly, shut up.

Joseph had seen the meanwhile of God in the Judean pit, in the plush home of Potiphar, in the midst of the strain of lingering temptation, and in the loneliness of a prison cell. By now, you have encountered the point and place of the meanwhile of God, whatever it is in your life that makes you uncomfortable or at least challenged. If you will lay aside the pride of life and your self-protectionist attitudes, you will be on the ride of your life as God begins to move.

When Joseph had the opportunity to self-aggrandize about his abilities, he chose to put focus on God. "I cannot do it," Joseph replied, "but God will give Pharaoh the answer he desires." And he reminded him two more times. Joseph refused the credit and placed all attention on God. Isn't that what God is after—our submission to his power? People say, "I can't get over the hurt, the disillusionment, the pain." Oh, yes, you can when his perspective dominates your experience and his power is sought. You don't have to buck up and bury the hurt. You say, "I can't, but God will." Those five little words will open up the treasure of the meanwhile in your life.

What a treasure for Joseph. Finally, this guy got a break. He informed Pharaoh of the impending famine, which was a bit of bad news, but he also gave a solution. The old saying, "Prepare for the worst and hope for the best," certainly applied to Joseph's advice. Pharaoh was struck by Joseph's words and proclaimed that God had made this known to Joseph and that it would be Joseph who would lead the challenge. Do you see how over the top this is? "You shall be in charge of my palace and all my people are to submit to your orders" (Genesis 41:40). There is a bit of irony in this because "all" would include Potiphar and Potiphar's wife. What a turning of the story. When God is on the move in our lives, the meanwhile becomes the impetus for his power to be seen. It gets even better for Joseph. The Bible says Pharaoh put a robe on him. I think that is just sweet of God.

In the last few years of my life, the pit, the prison, and the lingering moments of pain have all been experienced in this disease called Parkinson's. For me, it has been the meanwhile of God. There are moments that I digress into the thought that I have been forgotten by God and people. I know God hasn't forgotten, but the pain reminds me that it seems God no longer needed me in the game. So I sit on Sunday mornings in our church, listening to our pastor with Bible in hand, all suited for the occasion, and I sit ready to play, just hoping to hear God call me up to bat. Well, I am learning, a little bit at a time, that I am still in the game, but now with a different position. The other day, I read the book *The Sacred Journey* by David Cook. It is a book for golf lovers and tells the story of how a struggling golf pro revisits the foundations of the game for his personal survival. He had just lost his perspective of play, and his mysterious mentor reminds him that the tree, the bunker, or the wind are not his enemies on the course but are indeed his guide to take the ball where it needs to go.

It was five-thirty in the morning when it hit me. The truth of this unwanted disease, the meanwhile in my life, Parkinson's, had been seen as my enemy, my destroyer, the villain of my lost role in the kingdom. God was all over me at that point because I suddenly found myself referring to Parkinson's as my friend, my guide from God to take me where he wanted me to go and do what he wanted me to do. It had to be God because at five-thirty in the morning, I am normally not good for anything. I wept that morning because I realized how wrong I had been. God had not forgotten me or even taken me out of the game. He had just changed my position. It was up to me to shave and change clothes and prepare for the moment, the meanwhile of God. I had been living in the pit, the prison cell, and God wanted me in the palace. That morning, things changed for me. No…I changed. And after ten years of struggling with my newfound friend, I began to faintly understand the Father's choosing in my life.

The cold December morning when I was thirteen didn't end in the cold. Being forgotten led to me going to church with a friend of mine who invited me to come with him on several previous occasions. This Sunday morning proved to be the opportunity. As I sat, even at thirteen, intensely interested for the first time in what was being said, I found myself going to the altar and giving my life over to God, placing my simple faith in Christ. The meanwhile of God had been on the move in my teenage life, and this was just the beginning. I never returned again with Pop Stewart.

# Distance

There is a distance I fear
In this life of mine
That cripples my emotions
In this heart so sublime.
There is a closeness I've lost
To things I hold dear
And sometimes, I've wondered
If God is even near.
This dryness I have come to dread
As distance clouds this stormy head,
The moment is long,
The feeling is strong,
Who will rescue me
From this lingering bed?
Who then is this who steps into my fold?
I cannot see,

But wait; you'll hear
The voice I am told.
So with gentle words
And sweetened cords,
The closeness is restored,
And then I am told
With angelic accord
The voice has been the Lord's.

# The Meanwhile of Disillusionment

There is not a better way to start a day than on a freshly mowed tee box on a well-groomed golf course. My sports ability has always been in question, but when it comes to the game of golf, I have traditionally been proficient. Throughout the years of ministry, I have been privileged to know a number of PGA professionals, the closest of whom has been Bernhard Langer, two-time Masters Champion (and a host of other well-noted tournaments). If you are a serious golfer, you know the name Bernhard Langer.

What you might not know of Bernhard Langer is that he is a man who chooses to live in the meanwhile of God and thus, lives free of what he has and what he has become in the golfing world. He tells the story after his first Masters win in Augusta, Georgia, in 1985. The morning after the coveted win, he awoke to the image of the sterling silver detailed replica of Augusta's clubhouse and then the personally crafted green blazer that lay across the chair, both displayed prominently in his hotel room. His German stoicism led him to simply think, *That's it? This is the end of the road of emotions? Is this the pinnacle trophy of my career, a silver clubhouse and a green jacket?* Emptiness is all he felt. The experience was not what he had hoped for or expected. He was, you might say, disillusioned, but his disillusionment would lead to a week later giving his life over to the Lordship of Jesus Christ. He was left with the emptiness of the trophies of his prestigious win the week before and was now filled by the Holy Spirit of Christ. Many of us, if not all, experience moments of disillusionment when what we expected did not turn out the way we had thought. The hope for results did not come our way, whether it be via a sterling silver clubhouse—the promise of a well-deserved raise—or the expectations of a marriage or even a friendship. We all face moments when what we experience does not match our hopeful thoughts; we become disillusioned.

Even though disillusionment can come out of our deepest struggles or our most shallow thoughts, there is no doubt that it affects us long-term in how we handle life and what life throws at us. When life throws a curve at our otherwise peaceful and painless existence, we choose to become intensely bitter or deeply humbled, both of which impact our happiness.

Happiness? Well, that is a well-groomed motive for living. This passion for happiness becomes the hallmark of our emotions and, we think, the goal of God in the universe. One well-known Christian preacher and author has written a book on how to be happy seven days a week. I suppose he thinks that the goal of my life is to be happy and that the labor of God is to make sure I am.

Now, I'm not suggesting we walk around all day as if we had just swallowed a bottle of Pepto-Bismol. I am suggesting that God does not have on his A-list for today my personal happiness. God is not like the new parent who tiptoes in the house so as not to disrupt the sleep of the newborn. Notice that disillusionment comes when what we expected did not happen. The problem is not what has occurred but in our presuppositions about life. I have heard people say they are disillusioned with their marriage, their church, and even God. But why, we ask? Could it be that our disillusionment dominates because what we envision was wrong from the start? The problem does not lie within the marriage, the church, or God, but lies within ourselves. This truth cannot make its way into our lives until our lives hit a bump in the road, when we face unwanted pain, loss of a job, a break in a relationship, or any other drama. We are faced with a question of who God is versus who we have perceived Him to be.

Job describes it in Job 23:8–9, "But if I go to the east, he is not there; if I go to the west, I do not find him. When he is at work in the north, I do not see him; when he turns to the south, I catch no glimpse of him." Job is saying that he cannot find God on his own terms or within his whole perspective of who God is. The good news is God had found him in the midst of his pain. He continues, "But he knows the way that I take; when he has tested me, I will come forth as gold." Job understood the meanwhile of

God. The testing is still there, even when we cannot figure God out. Now, some of you will be going wild at the thought you don't have God so predicted that you can explain to others why they are suffering. We shudder at the thought that there is not always a verse that covers our pain. Sometimes, life leaves us holding the bag, wondering why. Within Job's struggle, he reveals the fact there is one who is not left in checkmate, and that is God. He knows.

But let's go back to our perceptions of God. We have created a polished model of God that responds to us rather than controls us. God wants us happy, so he frets over our comfort. He is the monopoly wizard who hands out blessings every time we pass go—our spiritual sugar daddy. This becomes a burden to carry because we are faced with keeping God's reputation clean and acceptable, so when we face pain, we smile with pursed lips or we blame it all on Satan. Somewhere in it all, we really think deep down that God owes us for our noble efforts. And so there is a secure blessing at the end of it all. There is no place for faith and trust within the meanwhile. The meanwhile is merely an intermission of life rather than part of the process of blessing. Just get to the end of the story of Joseph, the blessing.

Yet, Joseph was not disillusioned. I think we can learn a few things that will clear the way for God's purposes in our lives. Two essential parts to Joseph's moment with God are: the proper view of God and the right perspective of man about himself. To the enticing advances of Potiphar's wife, he would say, "Can I do this thing and sin against God?" Joseph recognized that he was the debtor. God didn't owe him; he owed God. And his obedience to the holiness of God was at the forefront of his life. God was not his protector from pain, but God was his sustainer within the pain, the problem, or the plot of evil.

I wish I could have seen that truth prior to my battle with depression, soon after the diagnosis with Parkinson's. The depression was crippling to my emotions because deep down I was saying, "God how could you? After all I have done for you?" Isn't that amazing? I believed I was in charge up until this crisis, which I blamed on a misjudgment of God, sort of a heavenly fiasco. Something had gone wrong in the war room of my life. Either that, or God was asleep and was left as much in the dark as I was as to what had happened to me. Of course I didn't say that. But it was the controlling thought. The more I tried to find God as Job did, the farther I would fall away. In those moments of depression, I had to be found by God and rest within that truth. My prideful self had to face off with the providence of God, and I was the one who had to wave the white flag.

It was Mother's Day eight months after the depression had swallowed my emotions and smothered my desire for God that the face-off came. We had been to church. Now that alone was a major step to a hurting pastor, but the pastor of the church was a close friend of mine in town. He was not consumed with fear over my plight. He kept saying, "This is just a season and not the whole story." One thing I will never forget was that he never made me feel ashamed that I, a pastor, was struggling with the truths I had preached. Pastor Bob walked with me through this time of my life and would prove later to be the initiator of my restoration. With his compassionate heart, there is no wonder that the church he pastors has grown to over 20,000 in attendance on any given Sunday. He remains to this day one of my dearest friends.

So now, back to Mother's Day. We came home with me so emotionally spent that I cried uncontrollably. My wife Linda had a great tolerance for my emotional outbursts, but this Sunday she had had enough. She politely told me she was taking the kids and going over to a friend's house for the rest of the day, and I, on the other hand, would remain home and work it all out. I agreed. As I lay there alone, I expressed my emotions with little restraint, *for I was alone*, I thought. No one was hiding in the closet. But the presence of God was so real that I began to physically shake. With desperation, I expressed my emotional disillusionment with God that he allowed this deep hurt in my life. *I had lost it all*, I thought—a promising career, a radio ministry, the involvement in so many outside causes, the traveling to Europe to speak and to teach, the respect of so many, and even the every Friday golf dates with the one I admired most in my life, my friend Gary. Gary was respected by all who knew him, but to me, he was the father I had always hoped to have. The loss of those times with him left me lonely and wanting.

On that bed that afternoon, God challenged me with acknowledging him as God and willfully trusting him for everything in my life. This was the showdown that had to come if I was ever going to be lifted from this black hole of depression. I quickly said, "Yes, Lord, I will." The moment I said that, a wind passed over my body that was real and undeniable. It was, in fact, the spirit of God. You may choose to reject the manifestations of his spirit, but I'm telling you, it was real. Something happened to me in that moment, for I've never taken another pill for depression since that Sunday afternoon on Mother's Day. I hesitate to share that for fear, you may think there is no place for medicine in helping people cope with depression. Please, if you suffer from depression, don't stop medication because of my experience. And don't carry the guilt that your faith is not strong enough. This is the way God worked in my life. In the following weeks, my mind returned to me, and I began to regain my emotional control. And God began to reveal the meanwhile of blessing.

What am I trying to say? There are moments of disillusionment that cross our lives that are brought on by our faulty view of God. God never promised us countless hours of joy, or he is obligated to give us lives of painless existence. I am not removed from the consequences of a fallen world. Well-behaved Christians get cancer, have car wrecks, and yes, are diagnosed with Parkinson's. I am called to see God as God, and that only one thing dictates his work in my life—his holiness, all expressed through his love for me. If you are in the meanwhile of being disillusioned, then you need to start here, by acknowledging that God is in total control, that you are in debt to his glory, and that his glory calls out the good for your life. As the Psalmist says in Psalm 16:6a, "The boundary lines have fallen for me in pleasant places." Joseph was spared disillusionment because he acknowledged the holy control of God. He would remind Pharaoh that God would give the meanings of the dreams and not him. And that leads to the second principle.

Joseph not only saw God but also saw himself as who he was. In his whole dialogue with Pharaoh, he never once took credit. He never once spoke of his track record or embellished his ability. He never drew attention to his unfair treatment by Potiphar or his abandonment by the cup bearer's forgetfulness. He had every right to promote himself and live in the moment. Joseph chose to live in the meanwhile. I'm sure he was the last one to expect what would come out of Pharaoh's mouth and the last one to see his newfound role within Egypt.

Wouldn't it have been tragic if Joseph had thought about how God had used him in the past? He had been the favored son, the most eligible bachelor, the fashion trendsetter with his love for coats. God had other plans. But it would take a pit, a persecution, and a prison cell to bring the palace to Joseph. Joseph was not the copilot on his journey. God alone was the pilot, and he was the passenger.

I know that is a challenge to us within ourselves. I couldn't count the number of times I have said, "God, used to use me in the pulpit, the radio, and in countless lives," until one day, God reminded me that I could live in the "used to's" if I wanted to. But if I did, I would miss it. He had and has a new work for me, and without the meanwhile, I would never know it.

The reality of that occurred recently when I was asked to be a deacon in my Baptist church. I was ordained a Presbyterian minister. I found myself wondering what a Presbyterian minister was going to do as a Baptist deacon, as if this was some lower role of service. The Lord gently reminded me that he had not called me to be a Presbyterian minister or even a Baptist deacon. He had called me to be his servant foremost of all. If this new role is where he wants me, then hold on to your seat, Michael, because he is about to do a new work and it will be exciting. Meanwhile, God has a plan. No room for disillusionment.

I have had the privilege of being in Bernhard Langer's home on several occasions. In his living room, you will find a few scattered pieces of past victories, which includes the sterling silver Augusta clubhouse, and the green jacket hangs in his private locker back at the Augusta clubhouse. What stands out the most is that the same living room has hosted countless Bible studies for young golfers and those seeking to know more of God. That same room has hosted the message of the Gospel and times of intercessory prayer and the bestowing of gifts to people in need. What you will hear there is the voice of Joseph. "I can't, but God can." No room for disillusionment.

# Observing the Sky

The layers of pillowed white
Stretch across the evening sky
And in the distance
Sudden light claps in rhythm
And then appears in stillness to lie
The host of rays from the awaiting moon
Beckons the night
And leaves the observing soul
Filled with its unheard delights
There is a presence beyond what is seen
And is known by only those
Who are willing to lean
For in the span of time
Somewhere in heaven's space
God lays out his plans
That only he can trace
And those who yield to what his drawing demands
Will find comfort within His creative hand

# The Meanwhile of Decision Making

For some, turning twenty-one means showing your ID and proving you are legally able to take your first drink. To Anthony Rossi, turning twenty-one meant leaving your family of nine brothers and sisters and landing on Davis Island in the New York Harbor in 1921. Anthony Rossi was born in Messina, Sicily, on September 13, 1900, and made a decision to come to America. He came with the intent of raising money for a film-making trip to Africa. But that decision would prove to fail; this left him driving a cab in New York City. By 1941, he sought to move to Florida and become a tomato farmer. Unsuccessful, he moved to Bradenton, Florida, and opened up a restaurant that soon reproduced itself in Miami. The negative impact of rationing during WWII closed the restaurants, and Rossi was unsure which way to go. He decided to get involved with the Florida citrus industry, and by 1947, he found himself selling gift baskets of fruit to major department stores like Macy's of New York and eventually supplying the famous Waldorf Astoria with one thousand gallons of fresh orange juice per week. He was the first to patent refrigerated trucks, which led to a mile-long train, carrying one million gallons of juice weekly to the New York City area. In 1957, a ship called the *S.S. Tropicana* was added, carrying 1.5 million gallons from Florida to New York; thus, the birth of Tropicana orange juice. In 1978, Anthony Rossi sold the juice empire for five hundred million dollars, a long way from the cabs of New York City.

It is a story of decisions; some were successful and some failed, but all served to produce the whole, story of a God-directed success. This success would be used to fund extensive evangelism in Italy and missions all over the world because Rossi's greatest decision was to give his life to Jesus Christ and live for the glory of God. When Anthony Rossi moved to Florida, he thought it was to make his fortune in tomatoes, but God had oranges in his mind. When he decided to open restaurants, God had in mind to supply orange juice to thousands of restaurants, and when Anthony Rossi decided to come to America in 1921 to raise money for a film career, God had in mind a citrus domain.

When Joseph decided to take his brothers a boxed lunch, God had in mind the feeding of a whole nation and generation of people. What happens in the middle is the story of the meanwhile. At every turn, Joseph was the initiator and oftentimes the recipient of short termed decisions, but with far reaching eternal impact. That is how God works. He works through us to position us, to guide us, to break us, to bless us, to teach us, to show to us his glory, and to reveal to us his plan. And he does it all through the decisions we make and our responses to the decisions of others. We normally have what we think is a clear picture of the future or at least a reasonable one. We feel safe because we can manage most of what we decide or we wouldn't have decided it. Most people agree with our decisions, and if they don't, we may rethink them. Our decisions are mostly self-serving and guarded by the thought of what will affirm us most in life. In the end, we pray for God to bless our decisions so we can stand with the greats and say, "The Lord led me," or something to that effect.

But what if God was so much in control that even our decisions were vehicles for him to shape our lives and use us without us knowing we were being used? What if God was so wise to guide the timing of our decisions and to use the motives behind our decisions to bring about his plan? What if God was so loving to turn our bad decisions into profit for our lives? And what if God was so graceful to even use our failure to display his glory? Well the good news is, God is all those things and more. And because he is, he wants more of our attention in the process of making these decisions. He is not interested in putting his okay onto our best laid plans. He wants us to see that while you and I may decide on something to say, to do, and to be. He is working out a more far-reaching plan than we may ever imagine. There is always a meanwhile.

Now, God is not dependent on our decisions to execute his will on Earth, but he does seem to use our decisions to reveal his will through us. This puts a new weight upon our own decisions and brings seriousness into our actions as well as an excitement. My decisions and choices, as limited as they may be, take on an eternal dimension, fueled by the very notions of God. If I sense the very presence of God in the smallest of decisions, then I learn the pure freedom of living within the boundaries of his plan. And when his plan is not clearly known, thus I live by faith.

The practical questions come such as, is God involved in my deciding where to park my car in a parking lot or which set of clothes I choose to wear on any given day? Do I choose to wear blue because God likes blue and therefore, he agrees? Or am I on my own? What we really want to know is, does God micromanage our lives and is that what walking by his Spirit means? If you are stuck here in those perplexing questions, it may be the reason for your never seeming to decide on anything and therefore living nonproductive lives. In the bigger picture, God is present, and my recognition of that truth frees me to live within the boundaries of his will, guided by his law, and empowered by his control.

What does the meanwhile have to do with my decisions? The complex answer is our decisions become the conduit through which God reveals his plan and makes his will known. I may think something to be God's will, but I don't know completely for sure until after it comes to be or not be. Up 'til then I hope and aggressively act upon that hope. The meanwhile takes us beyond the finiteness of my decisions and reveals what God is doing in the bigger picture of life. The Master's stage is always dominant, and we are the supporting cast.

So, to be faithful, do I pray for parking places? Yes. Why not? You may be parked beside someone who happens to say something that triggers a response in you and the next thing you know, you're sharing the Gospel. This person comes to Christ, and today, he or she is smuggling Bibles into China's underground church. Whew, all that from a parking space. Could it happen? Of course it could. But then again, I may choose the space just because it is the nearest to the store I could get, and that would be all right with God. Does that make sense? If it does, then you know what the meanwhile is all about. If it doesn't, then just relax, because it will.

There are several factors I want us to consider. First, *God uses our decisions to position us in order to guide us.*

In Genesis 45:25–28, Jacob, now named Israel, had to decide if he was going to pack up his family and make the journey down into Egypt with hopes of seeing his thought-to-be-dead son, Joseph. In his decision to go, he had no plans to stay, yet God, beyond it all, had other plans in place. God was working to get the whole nation of Israel down into Egypt. God was writing the drama of his glory. What Jacob believed to be a mere weekend reunion was indeed the positioning of God's people. The implications are overwhelming.

When I graduated from seminary, I had two very attractive offers of places to go for ministry. While Rock Hill, South Carolina, was not exactly a location draw. It was only twenty-five miles from Charlotte, North Carolina, where I grew up. The other opportunity was Tampa, Florida, to a broken church and less money offered per year. The advantage was, however, it was near the beach, and I love the beach. I ultimately chose Tampa. What I didn't know was that God was positioning me to fall in love with Linda Bardin, and the rest of the story is the meanwhile. God's guidance came by my decision based on ministry opportunity, but God had a plan of romance that has lasted, as of now, twenty-six years, and we have three beautiful children to show for it. God has a sense of humor because our age difference is eleven years, and little did I know that when I was praying in my junior year of college for my wife, God was positioning her in the third grade in Tampa, Florida. The meanwhiles can be interesting and fun.

Second, *God uses our decision to position us in order to break us.*

When Jacob made the decision to take his family to Egypt, he stopped in Beersheba to worship the Lord. God told him his far-reaching plan to make a great nation of him and his descendants. Genesis 46:3 words it like this: "Do not be afraid to go down to Egypt, for I will make you into a great nation there." The short-term effect was to be reunited to Joseph, but the long-term effect was that in the heat of the Egyptian desert, God would form a nation of people he would call His own. There in the restraints of slavery, God would birth the freedom call to mankind. God was on the move, but Joseph would perceive a practical problem during the extreme days of the famine. The people could not handle the tax burden owed to Pharaoh because there was no revenue available. Joseph offered money for the purchase of their livestock to cover their tax burden. When the second year came, the need was so great that the people offered their land and themselves in turn for money to buy food. Genesis 47:21 says that at that point Joseph reduced the people to servitude. In that one decision, Joseph set the framework for God to break the people of Israel so that they could see his mighty power and his eventual deliverance, which would foreshadow his redemption of man. Joseph, no doubt, thought he had settled a very complicated issue for the people, but in fact only created a slavery that would break them. Meanwhile, God had a plan that would make a far greater impact than merely settling a tax debt.

Never would I have thought that God would use Parkinson's disease to break me until I truly depended on him for everything. I believe that most Parkinson's patients battle with a feeling of worthlessness in daily life. The fine motor skills that are needed for swallowing, blinking your eyes, or picking something up off the counter is severely restricted. Your tongue becomes unable to properly say the words you are used to saying with a natural flow, and for a preacher, that is a frustration that is hard to articulate in writing. As I have told my wife on a number of occasions, "I can't think right now, so don't ask me questions." Your mind becomes so consumed with trying to say the words that you forget how to put the words together and then confusion sets in. Communication has always been important to me, and to not be able to communicate has indeed been the breaking of my life. Within this lofty act of God, God has given me a deeper insight into hurting people and has led me to experience what truly is of value to him. Yes, God is in the meanwhile, and I can say with confidence that there is no greater place to be than in the middle of the meanwhile.

Third, *God uses our decisions to position us in order to bless us.*

To be honest with you, there are days in the middle of this challenging experience of Parkinson's that I wonder where the blessing is. There are days that I indeed doubt that there is any blessing at all. Of course, that leads me down a slippery slope of emotions that always seeks to bury me under its landslide. But isn't that what it means to live in the middle of the meanwhile with God? The moving back and forth from my experience and the character of God is a mighty force of emotions, and the dynamic of its power depends on what I choose to yield to at any given moment. There are moments I want to curse it all. And there are other moments I want to embrace this unwanted friend of Parkinson's because God has used it for good somehow. I am learning slowly that the more I yield to him, the more I am positioned for blessing.

Joseph's whole life was about the positioning power of God. From his pilgrimage from the pit, dug for him by his brothers, to the palatial walls of a secured palace in Egypt, Joseph was positioned by God. Somewhere along the way, Joseph married and had two sons, Manasseh and Ephraim. The Eastern custom would mandate the passing along of blessings by the patriarch of the family. Joseph's sons were to be no different. Genesis 48:12 and following tells us that Joseph brought his sons to Jacob and positioned them according to what custom demanded the younger Ephraim on his left and Manasseh, the oldest, on his right. The positioning on the right side was symbolic of power and authority. By Joseph's arrangement, Manasseh would hold the dominate blessing for he was the oldest, but Jacob made a decision, and verse 14 tells us that Jacob crossed over and put his right hand on Ephraim's head and his left hand on Manasseh's head, switching the order of blessing according to custom. This must have looked like an Eastern version of the game Twister. It was very obvious and upsetting to Joseph, but despite his objection, the dominate blessing was given to Ephraim. What is interesting to me and worth noting is that Jacob had some inside desire to see the younger succeed. He himself was the younger and stole the birthright from his brother Esau. He wanted only the younger sister Rachel over Leah, the older sister. He had affection for the young. In the midst of this cultural confusion, Jacob promised

Joseph that Manasseh would be great as well, but there was no doubt the dominant line was given to Ephraim. Was this the case of Grandfather Jacob's confusion or was it intentional? Jacob knew who he was choosing. But in a greater way, God knew what he was orchestrating, a classic meanwhile of God— the human element being guided by the heavenly order, all for the purpose of blessing. As you follow the biblical development, God brings his blessing on Ephraim. Joshua 17:14 says that the people of Ephraim said, "We are a numerous people, and the Lord has blessed us abundantly." Both Ephraim and Manasseh drove out the Canaanites from the Promised Land. While Jacob planned the blessing, God was working to provide a protection over Israel. Through their military dominance, Israel would be positioned to take the land and inhabit it. The meanwhile made room for the blessing of God.

As I look back on my decision to accept the offer to minister in Tampa over Rock Hill, I see similar principles as those with Jacob and his grandsons. Tampa was the farthest away from home, the least paying, and yet would be the most demanding of my time and talents. I made the decision to go to Tampa because this would be the better learning experience, plus I loved the people. God, however, had so much more he would reveal in time. The greatest indeed was leading to the woman I fell in love with.

I met Linda Bardin my first official night with the youth ministry. A scavenger hunt had been planned and she and her best friend Kelly had strategically planned to ride with me. The fact that I had a new

Chevrolet Monte Carlo did not hurt the fact that I was somewhat popular as the new young minister. The evening event ended and we said good night. I know it sounds like a made for television movie, but that night, I fell in love with Linda Bardin. There was only one problem: we were eleven years apart in age. I quickly dismissed the feeling and did not revisit it again until three years later. I was the youth pastor and this could be my downfall if I acted on those feelings. To say I suppressed them is a little dramatic and elevates the feelings to more than they were at the time. Nevertheless, boundaries were set in my heart and mind, and by God's grace, I stayed within them.

In the fall of Linda's senior year of high school, we were attending a Sunday night Bible study in a mutual friend's home, independent of one another. During the prayer time, Linda began to cry, so afterwards, I called her aside for a moment and asked if there was something wrong that I could help her with. After all, I was the youth pastor. She confidently responded with, "I just can't tell anyone how I feel." At that moment, the tide of emotions I felt for her flooded my heart. The tension of being true to my heart and doing what was appropriate battled against me. I had never given any reason to her to think that I was interested in her, yet deep down, I knew she was talking about me. I resisted the urge to come forth and told her that we should not talk about our feelings now, but one day, we might. She assured me she would wait. That night, with that brief conversation, changed our whole relationship.

I never dated another girl, and neither did she date another guy. I am sure she turned down a lot of offers for relationships, but God had another plan in the works. We did not start calling one another or sitting with one another in church. In fact, we did not speak of it for the next six months, until after she graduated. We just knew God was at work in the meanwhile.

We are not sure when our first date was, but we believe it was some time during the summer. I had moved out of youth work into other areas of ministry, a strategic career move and a wise one at that. With the support of our families and church family, we were engaged in the spring of the following year and married by July. We just celebrated our twenty-eight anniversary, and I often look back and think that I had moved to Tampa for job-related purposes and my love for the beach, but God had a blessing much more significant than the beach. I shared my feelings in a poem I wrote on our nineteenth anniversary. The blessing of the meanwhile never ends.

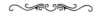

## Memories of Her

I am staggered by her face
As I behold the beauty of her grace
And her eyelids that fall
As if they upon her face do crawl.
The softness of her skin
Causes me to begin
Down a journey so unique

That causes me to retreat
Into memories that began
When I did place upon her hand
A pledge that only she would understand.
Into my life she birthed a son, and then one more
Then the years passed through our door,
Until arrived one so sweet
Who follows naturally within her feet.
Our journey has been kind, sometimes hard
But always strengthened by the power of his guard.
There have been moments of great relief
And then times that caused us grief
Yet made hopeful by deep belief.
And now pictured within this frame
A love that is captured by the reflection of his name
Within two people that remain
Still committed in this late refrain.
I am still staggered by her face
And the years of seasoned grace
She stands there still
As we walk life's hill.
She raises me up while on her knees
As we face the waves of stormy seas.
And as we pilgrim through this land,
Never removed from his hand
We see those birthed at home
Begin to venture into their roam.
So with satisfaction rare
Our memories are not bare
Painted by the stroke of his hand
With colors blended by his demand.

Fourth, *God uses our decisions to position us in order to teach us His character and glory*

I forget easily. It has something to do with Parkinson's, but I am afraid this was a flaw long before I was diagnosed. It seems that the spiritual lessons I am taught repeatedly in my life are the ones I should have mastered long before now, the basic ones like God is always in every place present, His omnipresence, and His knowledge of every moment of my life, His omniscience. Nothing takes Him by surprise. But there are moments I just forget and head out on my own and expect to win the day.

Joseph's brothers forgot all the unmerited favor shown to them by Joseph as they came down into Egypt. They had to be taught once again the reality of how God was protecting them. They thought that since their father Jacob had died, the penned up bitterness would be let loose on them. But there was no bitterness in Joseph and their fear was unfounded. Joseph was so aware of the presence and knowledge of God that God used that awareness to be guiding principles in Joseph's reaction to his brothers. Joseph's brothers, however, had not yet dealt with their guilt and certainly did not live by God's presence and knowledge. They were positioned for defeat and so are we if we fail to learn the character of God in the waiting periods of our lives. How much more exciting it is to live within the frame that God knows your needs and promises to never leave you stranded?

It was a couple of Christmases ago that I sat down to pay out our monthly bills, and in doing so I realized that if I tithed there would not be enough money for Christmas. So I held back the tithe amount, much to God's displeasure. Would I trust Him? Would God not let me off this one time? After all, it was Christmas. The thought of very little under the tree for my family was not an option. As the Sunday before Christmas approached, the Lord began to speak to me about the tithe money, but I stubbornly held on to my desire until that Sunday morning. I would trust Him, but not without holding Him responsible for taking the only money I could see that could be used for Christmas. Somewhere in my discussion with Him, He impressed on me the phrase "fourfold," that God would bless fourfold. I took the check and placed it within the envelope and waited for the offering to be taken. I had even taken a blank check with me just in case God would change His mind and I could give less. I placed the envelope into the offering plate as it was passed, but with mixed emotions of faith and doubt. *It is up to you God*, I thought. And I was right. It was up to Him. And when we leave it up to Him, we can trust that meanwhile, He is providing in a way that goes beyond us. After church was over, I saw a man whom I knew had supported my ministry in the past.

"Hey, Merry Christmas," he said. "I decided to give you my yearly giving to your work up front this year and not monthly, if that's ok."

I nervously opened the envelope, and in it was a check in the amount of fourfold as to what my tithe was just an hour earlier. While I was struggling in obedience, God was in the meanwhile and His presence and knowledge of my need was made very real to me. We went Christmas shopping the next day.

Fifth, *God uses our decisions to position us in order to reveal to us His greater plan*

Don't you just love it when you know something that no one else knows? You feel powerful, special, and important. You become the guardian of a potential surprise. You might feel a little guilty if you know something you should not know. It is exciting to think that we know the latest scoop and no one else does.

Joseph knew something the brothers did not know. He knew and lived by God's character. He knew God was the initiator of the events of his life and therefore would also be the sustaining power in the midst of life's struggles. This caused him to live not free from pain, disillusionment, worry, doubt, and bitterness, but a life empowered by them. He saw himself under authority. He was not consumed with personal comfort and having everything neatly explained. He was free to wonder about God and to explore God's ways. He asked almost a rhetorical question in Genesis 50:19, "Am I in the place of God?" The implied answer is no. He answered his brothers' fear of revenge by assuring them that he had no right to act revengeful because God had a plan to use their ill intent for the larger purpose of saving a nation and preserving the promise of God's covenant (Genesis 50:24). It is amazing that when Joseph had the opportunity to inflict a little sibling revengeful pain, he chose to reassure them and speak kindly to them. This was made possible because he had lived a life under the plan of God. He lived a life in and of the meanwhile. He maintained a view of God that was bigger than he was. God was not merely his best friend, the neighbor next door, or his sensitive care giver. But God was his God.

There is a side note here. If you are in the meanwhile, and chances are you are, then understand that Joseph's readiness to view his circumstances as God directed came quickly because he had a long-standing obedience to God and not a whim of faith. This was a lifestyle for Joseph and not a quick manufactured experience. It is never too early to begin to see God like Joseph and apply this perspective to your life.

Joseph saw beyond the immediate result of his choice to follow the plan of God. He saw the eternal plan. The apparent result was the well-being of his brothers and food for the nation. The far reaching result was the continuance of the covenant promise given to Abraham (Genesis 50:24). Joseph's decision to go beyond his pain and to live within the meanwhile set him free to live in peace with his God, his life, and with his relationships. His decision would give the beginning paragraph to God's drama that was yet to be written.

In 1913, Emily Dick filled in for her sister who taught a Sunday school class in one of the mill villages in Columbia, South Carolina. She maintained a burden for the spiritual needs of the mill village. So, after attending Moody Bible Institute in Chicago, she returned to Columbia with a vision for a similar Bible institute in the South. By 1918, Emily Dick and her friends, Margaret Childs and Mary Dibble, began praying for God to raise up a leader to bring a Bible training center to Columbia.

In the meanwhile, God had given Robert C. McQuilkin a vision to go to a foreign field and serve as a missionary. But the ship he had booked passage on burned in the New York Harbor, and God redirected his plan. By 1921, McQuilkin had joined the influential Sunday School Times and become a well-known preacher throughout the East Coast. After his third visit to Columbia, he was approached by the praying group of women in Columbia to come and help them start Columbia Bible Institute. McQuilkin prayed and sensed something special in this calling and moved to Columbia, and by the fall of 1922, classes were offered in a rented room in the Columbia YMCA. It was suggested to change the name to Columbia Bible School, and a year later, in 1923, Columbia Bible School officially began in two rooms in the Colonial Hotel. In 1929, the school offered its first bachelor's degree and the name was changed again to Columbia Bible College; today known, eighty-nine years later, as Columbia International University. Little did Emily Dick, Margaret Childs, and Mary Dibble know that their decision to start a Bible training school in Columbia, South Carolina, would be the provider for worldwide ministry, impacting millions of people over this last century. As they prayed in Columbia in 1923, meanwhile, God had a much greater plan.

Now in 1977, a young aspiring preacher in training made friends with Mary Dibble and Margaret Childs. He became the designated driver for the two praying founders as they attended the college's board meetings throughout the year. They would always ask him to join them in their prayer time upon arrival, and he always accepted. There would be a mysterious presence in those prayer times that would change this young man. It was there he learned the power and intimacy of prayer. They would be praying, and without notice, Margaret Childs would interrupt Mary Dibble and say, "Oh, Mary, now thank the Lord again for the gift of the red carpet in front of Dr. McQuilkin's pulpit. Thank him, Mary." And Mary would redirect her words and do just that. It was there that the young man first stood on holy ground and saw the value of decisions made with God's eternal plans in mind. Little did this young man know that at the age of forty-five, he would sit in a stoic hospital room and be told he had Parkinson's disease. The intimacy of those prayer times would give me the strength to rest upon the meanwhile of God and to trust him that he would use this Parkinson's for his glory in some way, somehow, in some time, with somebody.

You may live there today, as you read this book. I think we all live here from time to time. Decisions are made throughout the day as to where we go, what we do, and who we will be. Why not start, if you don't already, making decisions with a view of the eternal, so that when God writes in an intermission within our day, we remain seated and wait for the meanwhile of God to guide us, teach us, bless us, show to us His glory, and reveal to us his plan.

## Again

Something died
Within my soul
The moment I learned
My body was no longer whole
The wound dug deep
Within my mind
And my emotions
Were left stiff and blind
I could not see beyond the day
And I struggled to see
God's perfect way
Now time has past
Since I walked through pain's door
But even now my emotions still
Exist as numb and have yet to completely soar
But God is still God,
And I am still his
For my soul once died,
Has now begun to live…again.

# Living within the Moment

One thing that angers me about the evangelical church today is that we celebrate the blessing of God at the end of the struggles of life and not in the process to the blessing. Christian bookstores are filled with books about people who fought and won whatever their meanwhile was—everything from weight loss to moral failure, from financial disasters to lifestyle choices, and from health challenges to relationship crises. We celebrate and write about our happiness now that God has seen us through our time of darkness, dryness, and dread. They write with the sincere hope that you and I will learn from their failures. But what I want to hear and read about is how to live in the moment, your moment—when the meanwhile surrounds every turn of your existence, when your meanwhile seems terminal and the hope for a silver lining of God seems far removed.

How did Joseph do it? How did he make it without the Dr. Phil of his day or the noted preacher who tells you to live like everyday is Friday? How on earth could Joseph ever have gone from prison to palace, from prisoner to prime minister, without "claiming the victory" or "sending in his seed gift"? How could Joseph experience total peace and freedom without "letting go and letting God"? If I seem cynical, I am. These moments of enlightenment only seem to come after God has blessed us and removed the cloud from our lives. But, what about now? Right now, when the chemotherapy is not working? Right now, when he or she is not committed to making the marriage work? Right now, when the job is not restored? Right now, when the child has not turned his life around and is on his way as a missionary to the inner Congo of Africa? Right now, when life is not working for you and God seems to be distant? How do you live within the meanwhile? Oh, we give God time, but there is a huge difference between being fashionably late and just plain not showing up. Do we ever stop to remember that God does not have to show up because he never left?

You will notice one outstanding factor in Joseph's journey of life: he never, from what we know, had to go through being restored. The Scriptures do not speak of a restoration period. He endured the pit, fought off the temptation, lasted through being forgotten in prison, got beyond the bitterness of revenge, forgave when it was hard, and looked beyond the moment of the hurt. I am glad for that. I think that without his track record, we would try to justify our lack of spiritual stamina. But with it, we are challenged that living *through* the meanwhile only comes when we are living *in* the meanwhile. The book of our life is written within the midst of the pain, the doubt, and the need. This, my friend, is the authentic faith for which the world is thirsting. So how did he live within the moment? Two overriding traits in Joseph's life lead to two truths: standing in the sacredness of God and settling in the sufficiency of God.

We have already seen how *standing in the sacredness of God* is the impetus behind our stability in the midst of temptation. Here, I want us to see it as one of two lanes in which our lives should run their course. As noted earlier, Joseph said to Potiphar's wife, "I cannot do this thing and sin against God." Joseph was aware of and lived in the atmosphere of God's holiness and honor.

I have met people of importance before. I have had access to the governor of the state in which I lived and have had dinner in the governor's mansion. On those occasions, not one time did I ever feel the need to feel uncomfortable or remove myself or that his presence warned me of failure. When Peter saw the holiness of Christ and his power, he fell on his knees and cried, "Depart from me, Lord; I am a sinful man" (Luke 5:8). When I stood in Governor Beasley's office, I never felt as if I was unworthy; undeserving, maybe, but not unworthy. Joseph, on the other hand, was restrained and ultimately resisted sin in his life because he existed in the holiness of God. If Joseph had failed here, we might better identify with him, but we would not be challenged by him. He would become our partner in perversion, and not our mentor in mightiness. Joseph's obedience produced the fruit of seeing the good within his pain. His favor among men was a direct result of his honor to God and his favor from God. When we become insensitive to the holiness of God, we justify our sin and begin to believe that we are not so bad. After all, Jesus died for sin, we quip, as we stroll down life's path. Then the meanwhile of God enters our lives, and our coat is ripped off, and we wonder why. We fail to see and know and trust his plan beyond the moment because we don't recognize his present presence. God reveals himself in times of the meanwhile in order to call us to finish well. If you ever have been overwhelmed over the presence of God, you know exactly what Joseph experienced.

One Sunday in ministry, I had just preached on the ascension of Christ. At the end of the closing prayer, God whispered, "I am not done yet." I haven't finished. I was sensitive to that because my hope had always been to be part of a church where we worshipped until God was finished and not one in which the normal ruled: to worship until we were finished with God, or at least up to the moment the line at the K&W Cafeteria opened.

Then God made it very clear for me to take my shoes off and ask others to join me in light of the fact that we were standing on holy ground. It would be a gesture of our acknowledgement and not an act of sensationalism. On that day, God revealed his raw glory, and I never will forget that moment of ministry. To this day, I give credit to our people and our worship team who consistently led us all into the holy of holies of his earthly tabernacle. God never repeated that experience with us, but it was one time I was impacted by and opened up more to his spirit.

There have been times in facing temptation that the Lord gently reminds me, "Remember the shoes." I am able to live within the times of the meanwhile because I have known times of his moving. The meanwhile becomes worthwhile because he has made himself known. Joseph chose to stand in God's holiness and so must you and I. As a result, Joseph was able to live *settling in the sufficiency of God*.

Joseph was the first one to admit he had no natural talent to interpret dreams. He said to Pharaoh in Genesis 41:16, "I cannot do it, but God can give Pharaoh the answer he desires." This was all God, and there was no place for self-aggrandizing or embellishment of the gift God would give him. You can imagine the temptation this might have been. The spotlight was on him, and this was the one time to shine. This was his ticket out of prison. Little did he know just how out of prison he would soon become. God would be the one to rule the day, and God would do it. Joseph's life stood in the meanwhile because God was on the move in his life.

I think that in the midst of a complicated moment of our lives, we have a knee jerk reaction of wondering how we can fix things, how we can smooth things over. *Maybe we can borrow the money*, we think, *or change jobs or go to a different church*. All the while, God is seeking to show us his way of provision and his sufficiency for our lives.

I love movies. And some of the best times with my kids have been sharing moments of watching a good movie. The boys would plan boys' night out, and my daughter would look forward to date night. On one such occasion, the boys and I found ourselves at the movie *Little Giants*. It is the heroic movie of a ragtag football team in a small town put together with the weakest and least likely to play. All the players had been rejected by the more accomplished boy's team in town. The two coaches were brothers which added to the drama. A day was set for a championship playoff game. The contest was obvious with the polished team put together, organized, and groomed for greatness. The leftovers wore oversized uniforms as they slowly made their way to the field. Defeat was imminent. But as in any underdog movie, passion for the game kept them alive. On the final play of the game, Johnny, one of the smallest guys on the field, ran the ball. And just before his collapse, his father appeared at the end of the field between the goalposts on bended knee, with arms outstretched waiting for his son, and of course the winning touchdown. This is a movie, after all. At this point, I am in tears, with the boys, sinking deep into their seats. In fact, every time I see that movie, I cry at the same spot, and the boys, now men, say the same thing, "He's crying again."

What comes to mind is how often, when I am in the meanwhile experience with God, I want to take the ball and run with it. Just when I am emptied of myself and worn out from trying to make the blessing happen, God, my Father, bends down and empowers me to live one more minute with his control. He reminds me once again that he has a plan, and it will be good, even though I don't see it right now. He is my sufficiency.

A few months ago, my oldest son Trevor graduated from college and was offered the position of assistant professional at a prestigious golf club—his home course throughout his time on the golf team in college. One day, he called and told me of a member at the club who had inquired about his family and seemed anxious to meet us. The conversation quickly continued and nothing more was said about the man. A few weeks later, I would be on the phone again with him, but this time, I was going to have to tell him we just couldn't travel to be with him and celebrate his engagement to his soon-to-be fiancée Katherine. The money was not there for us to travel, something not uncommon in tough economic times. I dreaded the phone call and had prayed earnestly for God to open the way for us to go. I had determined that $250 would cover the trip, but if God wanted us to go, he would have to show me clearly because time was quickly passing. As I prayed sitting in my bedroom chair, the phone rang, and it was Trevor. My heart sank with an anticipation that we would not be going for the weekend.

"Oh, Dad, I wanted to tell you…you remember the man I told you about who inquired about the family?"

"Yes," I said, yet not very interested in the topic.

"Well, he handed me an envelope this morning with a note. And attached were two checks—one for my ring fund, and one for you, Dad, for $250."

Why? To this day, I don't know why. Why this day, this moment, and why me? I didn't even know this man. I sat, overwhelmed. God was in my meanwhile, and he was on the move in my life. I couldn't help but think about the day that we sat in the theater, watching *Little Giants* with Johnny's dad's outstretched arms. We packed the car and left by lunch.

## Honest Unsettledness

Do I dare to question why
Before the eternal throne on high,
Or do I quietly regress
Into the shell of my external dress?
Oh no, I must step nigh
And face the lingering sighs,
So that I may not digress
Into the tomb of shallowness.
Do I carefully wonder why
Before the One who sets the sky,
Or do I refuse to address
The depth of my distress?
Oh no, I must abide
Within the framework of my cries,
So that my life may now confess
A confidence in God's eternalness.
So, now I'll wait and see
Just what providence will do with me,
But the questions I hold so deep
Still disturb my soul in sleep.

# Winning the Battle of the Meanwhile

It was the 1996 baseball World Series. It was game seven between the Cleveland Indians and the Florida Marlins. It was the bottom of the tenth and South Florida night air was filled with excitement as to if the Marlins would break the tie. Edgar Renteria came to bat for the Marlins and hit a hard ball through Cleveland's infield to drive in Craig Counsell, who was on base for the winning run and the series championship. It was true. The Florida Marlins were the world champions. I sat in the first base infield box and felt it all. Frank Wren was the assistant general manager of the Marlins and a member of our church. Frank had offered me the tickets along with Jeff and Marsha, also from the church. And I wasn't going to pass it up. There is, after all, some benefit in being a pastor in South Florida. As you can imagine, there was uncontrollable joy when Renteria hit that line drive and Counsell touched home base for the win. We immediately jumped out of the box and onto the field, hugging everybody in sight. Women were screaming, men were hugging each other, and kids were running feverishly to players for autographs. It was a win to remember. The Marlins had not been expected to get very far that season, much less win the World Series. But there we were, being sprayed with champagne and putting on the coveted world champion hats, prepared beforehand in the hopes of winning. At that moment, winning was all consuming. I have a bat signed by Edgar Renteria and Craig Counsell, and every time I look at it, I relive that winning night.

There is something about winning that makes a person feel almost invincible. A confidence is found in winners that motivate them for the next time around. People like winners, and they like to identify with winners.

Joseph was a winner at every turn. We learn from Joseph's winning moments there is much to be explored as you move to the end of Joseph's life. From his successful leadership of Egypt through their national crisis to the private meetings with his unrepentant brothers, Joseph models for us how to win when life has suppressed every chance to win. You cannot read the drama of Genesis 42–50 without feeling the pain of a troubled family. The father Jacob is still grieving what he thought to be the death of his young son and is still dysfunctional with the raising of Benjamin as the new favorite son. The brothers had not conquered the guilt of the past and were still plagued by their actions years prior. And Joseph was in emotional crisis, weighing forgiveness against a natural reaction of bitterness and revenge; all this while the land of Goshen was in the midst of widespread hunger. Talk about an award-winning script for Steven Spielberg. These were just the mainline stories.

It could be debated that Joseph's solution led later to a government takeover and a loss of property rights of the people; all of this leading to the suppression and slavery of Israel by Egypt. Joseph was not perfect when it came to political management, but he was a master at relationships in crisis.

The meanwhile of God saturated the very core of Joseph's life at this point. And what we learn can be life transforming. My life was radically transformed by Parkinson's. Today, ten years after the diagnosis, I realize that if I had lived out the principles I had discovered, my life and the life of my family might be vastly different. Everyday, I live with the buried guilt of why I was not stronger as a man. Why did I allow the threat of exposure of my failures during depression rule the day? Why did I agree to quietly bow out of life and cut myself off from the people I loved and served? Why didn't I clearly see the meanwhile of God? How different might my life be? The answers I am not sure of. But beyond these damaging questions, there lies a meanwhile that God continues to use in order to keep me on the road of trusting him…really trusting him.

Perhaps you are there, anxiously waiting for God to make sense out of your confusing moments of life. How do you live like Joseph and win when losing has become normal and curiously comfortable?

## Forget and Forgive the Past

There is an intriguing verse in Genesis 42:21, "They said to one another, surely we are being punished because of our brother. We saw how distressed he was when he pleaded with us for his life, but we would not listen. That is why this distress has come upon us." The brothers were still haunted by their plot against Joseph. For more than twenty years, they could not close their eyes at night without seeing Joseph's face. Their regret, now years later, still overruled the peace in life. Their guilt had been hidden but not forgotten. Joseph, on the other hand, recognized them from the start, and no doubt felt some vindication that they now bowed down to him, just as he had dreamed some twenty years earlier—the dream that had started all this mess. Because we are on the other side of Joseph's meanwhile, we can see the why of God. But Joseph was in the middle of it, and all he had were some hungry brothers with a past. The Bible says, "He pretended to be a stranger and spoke harshly to them" (Genesis 42:7). This guy still could not get mad. Oh he remembered the dream, the torn robe, the bit and the chain of his slavery. He remembered the accusation of rape, the false imprisonment, the lonely days of being forgotten, the false hopes of being released, and forever living alone. Yes, he remembered. But unlike the brothers, he chose to forget the past. He chose not to bring up their sibling hatred and their conspiracy of evil intent. The Bible just says he remembered.

But how then did he forget? I think Joseph was so focused on the present reality of God's presence that he forgot about himself and saw himself as part of the larger plan of God. Every time I allow myself to focus on the Parkinson's, I digress into bitterness of past actions and words directed to me. The hurt and pain of feeling left alone bites into my soul. Even while writing this book, I have had to stop and choose to forget the past. But how do you forget the past when the past has directly affected the present? The fact is you can't forget.

How am I to forget the night I took Pris Wall to see the movie *The Way We Were* with Robert Redford and Barbara Streisand and then Pris broke up with me over pizza afterwards? Her actions were tender, but her timing was terrible. That's been almost forty years ago, but who's counting? Joseph just remembered, but he chose to act apart from his emotional scars, a choice only made possible by the present reality of God's presence and control.

If you are here, reliving the moment of hurt, the act of failure, the unjustified burden, the unwanted pain, the unfairness of the loss, and the undoing of your soul, then Joseph would shout with directness yet with compassion, "Get over it!" Choose to step out of the control of the moment. Remember, Jesus never asked Peter for an apology. Wow, now that hurts. But forgetting only comes when we forgive. I'm talking real, tested, and lived out, unconditional forgiveness. As with anything, forgiveness is a process and the lack of forgiveness only hurts those who don't. Think how miserable life would have been for Joseph if he would have waited around for his brothers to come to him with pleading hearts, begging for his forgiveness. There is not even a hint in Joseph's character that he struggled over the feeling of revenge. It was just not in his vocabulary. Granted, Joseph played somewhat with their emotions and tested their seeming humbleness, but you never hear him throw up the past or make a reference to his variety of challenges the past twenty years. Joseph reveled in his identity to them in Genesis 45 where the Bible says, "Afterwards, his brothers talked with him." I would have loved to have been a fly on the wall during that conversation. Talk about awkward.

It wasn't until after the death of their father Jacob that the brothers really came to the point of admission that they had ever done anything wrong. Even then, their words were shallow and without the owning up to their failure. They were not regretful, and their words were elementary. "Daddy told us to tell you that you should let bygones be bygones now that we are all back together. Daddy said we should ask you to forgive us, so we are asking." This was not exactly the environment for the healing of wounds deep seeded.

We have all been here, waiting around for someone to say, "I'm sorry." We have all wanted to have those who hurt us say, "You know I was wrong." This is the meanwhile I think is the hardest of all because it takes truly seeing God behind it all. Joseph, in true fashion, did not plead his case for their recognition of his hurt. He was silent. Why? How? All because of the providence of God. He trusted that God had a plan and in the meanwhile, he would live free and know the joy of living because at the end of the day, he had a nation to feed. Winning the battles of life always requires us to look beyond ourselves and even remove ourselves from the hurt. Only then can you forget. As long as the pain is allowed to continue, your emotions will never be free of the past, and you will never be open to forgive.

## Follow the Providence of God

The 1924 Olympic Games were held in Paris, France. It was the Olympics in which the famous runner, Eric Liddell, refused to run on Sunday, which later became the storyline for the movie *Chariots of Fire.* He was a hero for people with values. There was another hero during the 1924 Olympics, Bill Havens, who was to compete in the sport of crewing. He had won a variety of honors and was the expected gold medal winner for the American team. The Olympics would be his pinnacle moment. Days before he was to leave for Paris with the rest of the American team, Bill Havens learned that his wife most likely would give birth to their first child a lot sooner than they had first thought. If he went with the team to Paris, he most likely would not be home for the birth of their first child. Bill Havens had a decision to make. Should he stay the course and go on to Paris and win the gold, or should he stay home and have his Olympic dreams die? Well, ultimately, Bill Havens chose to stay home and be by his wife's side at the birth of their first child. His critics were indeed right; Bill Havens never made the Olympic platform and was soon forgotten…until 1952 when the Olympic Games were held in Helsinki, Finland. The American Olympic crew team had won a variety of honors. There was another American hopeful that was sure to bring home the gold. And as predicted, he did. And he remembered Bill Havens and quickly sent a telegram back to America with a note that simply said, "Dear Dad, thanks for being there when I was born. I am bringing home your gold medal." (If you are a crier like me, now is a good time to let it all go.) It would eventually all come full circle for Bill Havens. Can you imagine the joy that came his way when that telegram arrived twenty-eight years later? Meanwhile, he had been living life. I don't know what Bill Havens' spiritual life was all about. But I am sure he looked back and recognized that a larger plan had been in place all along.

That plan is called the providence of God. And if you are to live in the meanwhile and win, you must see your life as part of a larger plan. Joseph lived with confidence that God was always on the move and was always carrying out his plan, even if he seemed silent. When Joseph identified himself, his brothers must have reacted in complete shock before the fear set in. Joseph mentioned being sold into slavery two times, just in case they had forgotten. I have learned not to overlook the small print in Scripture. You can feel the tension in the room as Joseph reminded them of what they had done. This was ultimate vindication for Joseph. The Bible says, "And now do not be distressed and do not be angry with yourselves for selling me here." In other words, you did me a favor. While you have been back home rationing out food, I have been here having second helpings. Joseph then added, "Because it was to save lives that God sent me ahead of you." This is incredible. Joseph called being put in a pit and sold as a slave God's way of sending him ahead. And there it is again. The meanwhile of God sprinkled with providence.

Now, as I said earlier, I love to go see a good movie. I love especially movies that end well. You know the storybook type. I can't watch the movie *Rudy* without dreaming I'm on the field at Notre Dame, chanting his name or watch the film *Invictus* without wishing I had known Nelson Mandela and somehow being taken by Morgan Freeman's voice as Mandela. The movies *Braveheart*, *The Bucket List*, and yes, *Little Giants* are all known for the way they end. And so is this real-life drama in Genesis 50. You see, that's what the providence of God does. It tells the end of the story, even though the story is not over. The providence of God assures us that when it is all said and done, that when the book of our life is written, it will all be with two last thoughts—his glory and our good. This is the calling of the meanwhile. If I live with this as the theme of my life, then I will conquer the meanwhile. So when Joseph said, "You intended to harm me, but God intended it for good," you believe him and win.

I know what you're thinking right now. You're saying, "Yeah, but you don't know what I am going through." How do you possibly tell a young girl who lost her husband in Iraq that God meant it for good, or a young man his wife? How do you tell a young college student she isn't accepted into the college of her choice? How do you tell an employee he is no longer needed but that God will supply his need? We focus on saying the right words rather than focus on true compassion for those that are hurting. So many times we focus on scripted answers, our theological boundaries, our prejudices, and not people. We all face the meanwhiles with all different levels of intensity and reactions. How do you get through it and come out victorious? How do you live in them and not lose hope?

Joseph is the most hopeful guy you could ever meet in Scripture. God would indeed take the moments of doubt, pain, fear, and loneliness and pull it all together. One thing Joseph never lost was hope. I think this is the most damaging aspect of depression. The moment we lose hope, we abdicate any responsibility to trust God. If providence does anything at all, it provides a reason to look beyond the day, see God at work, and place an active faith in He who will not let us slip so far that we are forgotten. He knows and He is not silent.

Now, if we were real honest, we would also admit that you and I carry guilt at times that puts our life on hold because of some failure in our lives. We lose the confidence of any future with God or his Kingdom. The brothers of Joseph could not see the future as good because they had never faced their guilt. Even when they did, it was lame. But we wrongly think that if we deny and bury guilt, that God just acts like nothing is wrong. That way, God keeps a clean record, and we walk away free of shame. Providence allows us to admit, deal with, and rid our lives of guilt and walk with hope when we are in the meanwhile—when it looks like we will never see God work in and through us again. It is during the meanwhile moments of no hope that God renews and restores us to the future, but this, time his future and his dreams for us. Our dreams are never as good until they are allowed to die first and are given over to God. We simply must wait and see what he will breathe on and empower so we live out his dreams.

So can we admit that God is not in the business of helping us achieve our goals and make our dreams come true? What God is up to in the course of a day is seeing his glory to the end and for us to see we are all part of that plan. In order for us to see that, we must step aside and forfeit our pride, which leads us to the third principle.

## Forfeit the Pride of Life

I will never forget that night I heard about Mary Alice Hipp. Mary Alice had worked for a small Baptist church outside of Spartanburg, South Carolina, for forty-nine years. She retired the night Linda and I had gone to a concert in Spartanburg to hear the Brooklyn Tabernacle Choir. I was going through disappointments in my first senior pastor role over the church growth rate in our church in Greenville. You know, the awful thought that church growth meant bigger numbers every week. If not, we must not be marketing well enough, or it must be me. I missed my calling. But what would I do? Sell shoes at the local mall? I had gotten that far in the process. Now don't get me wrong. There is nothing wrong with selling shoes. I like shoes. It was just not my calling. God knew that, so that's why he had us at the concert. We thought it was just a break from the routine, but God, meanwhile, had a plan.

Before the concert began, they gave a local award away to one of God's servants in ministry. That's when she walked onto the stage. They praised Mary Alice Hipp for serving for forty-nine years as choir director. She politely accepted but before she walked off the stage, they asked her, "Why did you stop at forty-nine? Why not retire after fifty years?"

Her response was penetrating. "Well," she said, "God told me to stop, so I stopped." And she walked off the stage.

But God walked the truth right into my heart. "That's where you have missed it, Michael," he said to me, "You see Mary Alice Hipp? Life is not about her. It wasn't about her dream of serving fifty years as choir director. I told her to stop, so she stopped. But life is about you, your dreams, your career, your church, as if you just need me to bless and give you the go ahead."

Well, I started to cry. (*That figures*, you're probably thinking by now.) With all the compassion of a loving wife, Linda said, "Not here, not now. Do not cry on me. The concert hasn't even started." But God spoke to me that night that life was not all about me but about his plans, his promises, and his glory.

I never met Mary Alice Hipp. I suppose one day, I will meet her and I'll say, "You remember that night in Spartanburg?"

She will say, "I know. I was there."

God changed my heart that night and ever since then, every time I get into a meanwhile of life, I remember Mary Alice Hipp. You see, God doesn't want my tomorrows or my yesterdays. He wants my todays. I live in the moment because God is not terribly interested in my plans. Life is not about me.

Joseph's youthful spirit must have had some satisfaction when he communicated those dreams to his family. His satisfaction would soon turn to challenge. Over and over again, he had opportunities to take credit before Pharaoh for his talents to interpret dreams. He had the power to make the brothers pay for their evil plot against him. He could have had reasons to promote his agenda and take advantage of his power to avenge himself. But what did he do? He threw a reception for his brothers. He took the spotlight off of his pain and placed attention on God. This attitude set him free from self promotion, the natural tendency of man.

If you know anything about children's literature, you know the name Judith Viorst. Whenever I need a light moment, I turn to Judith Viorst. In her book of poems entitled, *If I Were in Charge of the World*, there is a poem called "Remember Me." It captures the heart of every person's need to be accepted and known.

## Remember Me

What will they say
When I've gone away?
He was handsome? He was fun?
He shared his gum? He wasn't
Too dumb or too smart? He
Played a good game of volleyball?
Or will they only say he stepped in dog doo at
    Jimmy Altman's party?

Can't you just feel it? We all want to look good in the eyes of others. We don't want to be remembered for our mistakes. Why? Because we live as if life is about us. When we bring that attitude into our lives, everything has to work in our favor. We call it pride, and pride was the core of the fall of man and has been at the bottom of man's problems ever since. Going through uncertain times causes us to deny ourselves and forfeit our pride so we may see clearly the God of the meanwhile who helps us to intentionally discover his blessing and purposes in our lives.

This is where I struggle so often. Parkinson's is a pride-breaker. It has taken ten years, but I am just now becoming comfortable with showing my symptoms publicly. I don't like it but it is becoming more a part of my life, and I don't have the emotional need to hide it any longer. The hand tremors, the leg stiffness, the eyelids falling, and the nervous sounding voice at times all used to silence me. But I can't always appear good for others. Even though I still try to dress sharp, I doubt I always appear sharp. I'm learning to let loose of the pride and live to enjoy the moment that God has given.

## Find the Place of Blessing

This fourth principle is simple and very practical. There is no doubt in my mind that Joseph had to carry the attitude that he would see God in everything within his life. He chose to not live in self-pity, disillusionment, and bitterness. He chose the freedom of seeing God behind it all. He lived there in that vein of life. It was God who would give Pharaoh the meaning of the dreams. It was God who would be grieved if he fell to the enticements of Potiphar's wife. And it was God who sent him ahead of his brothers to Egypt. What about you and me? Will we choose to live that way when faced with the reality of the meanwhile? Will common happenings in our day become part of the work of God to produce his uncommon story through us?

I suppose one person who has taught me more than anyone how to live like this is my mother. Now that my father has died, she lives with us. The other day, I took her to the grocery store. You have to understand that the grocery store is her place of dominance. She loves it. Put her in the meat department, and she is a happy woman. She purchased a turkey breast and was able to save over three dollars with her coupons. This, of course, is part of the hunt. When she checked out, they charged the full price, and she caught them. According to store policy, when overcharging the customer, the customer gets the item free. My mom walked away with a free turkey breast. My mother is eighty-eight, and she was talking later that day to her sister who is ninety. I heard her say, "Let me tell you what the Lord did today." *That's it*, I thought. Her winning faith was made real and authentic because she was able to see God in everything. Who knows…when you are in the middle of the meanwhile and your faith is dry and your emotions are stoic, God has a turkey breast waiting for you.

## Fasten your Seat Belts

By April of 2008, the Parkinson's had progressed to the point I had to put an end to public ministry. I sat in my neurologist's office, and he recommended that I go to Wake Forest University Hospital to consult Dr. Tatter about deep brain surgery (DBS). He thought that I was at that point, and this surgery had proven to be most helpful to Parkinson's patients to restore them to a more normal way of life. I made the visit to Wake Forest a couple of hours away and sat in Dr. Tatter's office. He was every bit the professional and uniquely qualified for this surgery, having served Harvard and having performed this operation at least two times a week over the previous ten years. The time was set. I would have deep brain surgery on April 8, 2008. My confidence was high, and my faith was boosted by the blessing of the greatest doctor that man could have delivered. God had surrounded me with the best, and Dr. Tatter remains one of my heroes today.

The morning came, and I made my way to the pre-op room where I was greeted by this caring doctor. I don't know what possessed me except the spirit of God, but I said to Dr. Tatter, who was marking my head for the screws of the halo to hold my head in place, "We should have a word of prayer." He agreed. I was at peace, but the thought of someone probing in your brain for five and a half hours, preceded by drilling two holes in your skull, was a little unnerving. I prayed, "Lord Jesus, may we have a worship service in the operating room this morning, all for your glory."

They wheeled me into the room where I was greeted by at least nine people. I was to be awake for the entire operation. Since there are no pain receptors in the brain, just numbing the skull was all that was needed in order to drill the two holes in my head. My wife now says it was to prove that I was officially a numbskull. My kids would say, "Dad has not one but two holes in the head." Who needs enemies when you have a loving family?

God had given me Psalm 16:5–6 as a promise: "Lord, you have assigned me my portion and my cup; you have made my lot secure. The boundary lines have fallen for me in pleasant places. Surely I have a delightful inheritance." I quoted it to my newfound friends in the operating room and said, "Now, let's worship the Lord." I preached. The preacher in me was not going to miss an opportunity to preach.

For five and a half hours, Dr. Tatter placed electrodes into my brain, and I continued to preach. Now I have to say that it was one of the greatest times of worship for me. God was in that room, and it has since proved true that DBS would be beneficial to me long-term. God was alive and well in my meanwhile. God took me back to earlier days when I first found out about having Parkinson's. He was at the core of my dark, day and he would use it all for his glory. A true contentment ruled my heart that God was at work and that I didn't have to win the meanwhile because he already had won it in Jesus Christ. The meanwhile is not the dry period. The meanwhile is when I am the most alive because I am actually forgetting and forgiving the past, I am following the providence of God, I am forfeiting the pride of life, and I am finding the place of blessing. The meanwhile is not the time to retreat and passively wait for God to intervene, but it is a time to fasten your seatbelt for God to reveal the journey of your life where the walk in God will be the clearest you will ever have. It is a time of realness. It will be a time of battle but not defeat, a time of damage but not permanent scarring.

In the last few years, a prominent seminary staff member referred to me as being "damaged goods." I was hurt by such an insensitive remark, but then I thought he was really paying me a compliment, that I was just like Jesus Christ. Christ was damaged goods but not defeated. He came out of his meanwhile victoriously, and because he did, so will I. And so will you.

# Trusting

I'd like to know the reason
And understand the whys,
Of how we go through seasons
And moments filled with cries.
I'd like to bury memories
That cause me not to sleep.
I'd like to take the broken dreams
And carry them to the deep.
I'd like to restore the shattered day
When numbness upon me fell.
I'd like to erase the fearful thought
That I remember so well.
I'd like to take the lingering pain
That upon my heart does swell.
I'd like to break the insecure thoughts
That hold me like a spell.
But time will heal this heart of mine
And hope will make secure
The peaceful days and rebuilt dreams
And pain I can endure.
So, I will trust the living God
Who knows the reason why.
I'll wait upon his guiding hand
And forever will abide.

# Afterword

The Meanwhile Continues: A Personal Note

When I was a little boy, Saturday night was a big night. The show *Perry Mason* came on followed by *The Hollywood Palace* variety show. We would all get our baths, prepare our snack of orange slices and those small bottled Cokes, and wait. There was a certain commercial that always seemed to come on, a Timex watch commercial that would test the endurance of the watch by dragging the watch behind a tractor or dropping it from an air balloon or putting it on a boxer's wrist. It would always end by giving the famous line, "It takes a licking and keeps on ticking." If there is anything that can be said about Joseph's life, it is that he took a licking, but he kept on ticking. The meanwhile just seemed to go on and on. Even when he died, his dying wish—to be buried back home—was delayed. God was working out his plan for Israel and paving the way for Moses and the great Exodus out of Egypt.

My pilgrimage in Parkinson's has been a continued meanwhile. The ever-growing symptoms of stiffness and rigidity and tremors and times when I can't walk or talk or even think, not to mention the punishing and often misunderstood side effects of the medication, all impact my life. The challenge to get beyond the circumstances of pain gets more challenging. What most people don't realize about Parkinson's is the emotional and mental pain it brings. The feelings of worthlessness are overwhelming. There are days that the medication works well, and I look like a healthy man, and people look at me and say, "I would have never known." I always feel obligated to explain to them the truth of my condition.

The hardest time of the week for me is Sunday mornings. I sit and listen to my pastor and think, *I used to do that and say that*, or *I would have done it differently*. I have learned not to hold those opinions too firmly because God is doing a new work in me. I thought he had stopped using me, because he was not working the same way as in the past. I can't say how much time I have wasted by being a prisoner to that way of thinking. I find that people mean well when you are in the pause of your life; when it appears that God is silent in your life. Others take that as an excuse to express their opinion of why God is allowing it in your life. I have been told everything from if I had the right faith, I would be healed to God is using this to be an encouragement to the church. Now, I love the church. But it would not have been my idea to be a poster boy of how to handle pain. I could have preached a well-organized sermon on the topic, and they would have been sufficiently blessed. It goes beyond me to see how others think that they are God's self-appointed prophets to your life when you are in the midst of displeasing times. What is even more amazing to me is the inability the church seems to have to comfort those who are hurting and questioning the ways of God. We feel like we have to rush the hurting souls through the pain so they can seize the victory and not be a black eye on our otherwise clean-shaven façade. We are afraid to say, "I don't know why, but I know who," and leave it at that.

I am learning on this never ending journey just how incredibly stubborn I am in my life, with my way, in my time, and on my terms. When will I just give it up? It would be easier if God had made a mistake. Then he could correct it, and everything would be back to normal. I have enough faith for that. But the real question is, "Do I have the faith to believe that God has allowed the Parkinson's, my meanwhile, and that he knows best, even to the end?"

"Really?" you say. "Does he really know best?"

Yes, he really does. I know. I am there—living in the meanwhile.